# YOUR UBER SALES CRAFT

A Comprehensive System to: Help your Sales Grow and Keep you Focused

Brian Gwyther

*This book is dedicated to my family for all their support
and to the healthcare world in which I've worked.*

Copyright © 2021 Brian Gwyther

All rights reserved

No part of this book may be reproduced, or stored in a retrieval system, or transmitted in any form or by any means, electronic, mechanical, photocopying, recording, or otherwise, without express written permission of the publisher.

# CONTENTS

Title Page
Dedication
Copyright
Introduction
You ............................................................. 1
Organise ....................................................... 7
USP ............................................................. 22
Rehearse ...................................................... 35
User ............................................................ 38
Behaviour .................................................... 47
Engage Strategy ........................................... 54
Rapport ....................................................... 57
Statement .................................................... 66
Ask .............................................................. 69
Listen .......................................................... 73
Explain ........................................................ 76
Summaries .................................................. 80
Close ........................................................... 84
Reinforce .................................................... 88
Agreement .................................................. 90
Follow up .................................................... 92
Testimonial ................................................. 94

# Afterword

## INTRODUCTION

I've worked in healthcare sales since 1987, as a 'Sales Rep' for over than 20 years and, more recently, as a sales manager for more than 10 years. I've wanted for a while now to write down my experiences to help others who may be starting out on their sales journey. My sales experience comes from within the Healthcare sector (NHS predominantly in the UK) and have worked for large companies such as Coloplast – Zimmer – Hill-Rom, within sectors as diverse as Ostomy & Continence to Neurosurgery. I've also started my own business as well as being involved in start-ups. From the Porter to the Director of Nursing and Consultants, we are always 'selling' or looking for a 'Win Win' situation with our customer. I currently manage a sales and nurse team and coach them to become better sales and clinical people, therefore achieving their sales targets and KPI's. I find this an interesting point though: no-one coaches a sales team for their sales target, it's important to achieve target of course, however; coach them to improve their sales skillset, their effectiveness, their confidence, their expertise, their opening statements, their value added explanations, their Needs Matching skills. Control the 'Inputs' and the 'Output' will take care of themselves.

Quite possibly, like me, you have attended a number of sales courses and have gained a lot of sales insight from them. Keep practicing the techniques you've learned and follow your processes to help 'close' customers or answer 'objections', after all, rehearsing and practicing your craft is vital. I don't see this system as a replacement for anything you have learned to this point: We're here to try to assemble, from my experience, the most comprehensive sales system for you, to examine yourself and your actions at each stage of a sale, in order to help you become as successful as possible. Controlling the inputs if you will.

The **'YOURUBERSALESCRAFT'** system will be universal to almost all sales processes, it's created within a useful structure to help check, prepare and enhance your sales activity.

I'm not a career sales trainer who hasn't really 'done it', I've been 'doing it' for over 30 years now. So my **'YOURUBERSALESCRAFT'** is pulling from my experience, with additional research from leading sales coaches and trainers, with a smattering of body language and behaviours thrown in for good measure. In addition, I wanted the system to be able to be referred to, like a dictionary, so jump in to an area where you need some help and I hope you find the answers you need. This is the point of - **YOURUBERSALESCRAFT**, to better help you achieve your success. It's also written by me, in my own way and I usual don't 'fluff up' my words, keeping things as direct and to the point as I can. I hope you get some useful tips from the book and it helps you to become successful in what you are looking to achieve.

## YUSC Graphic

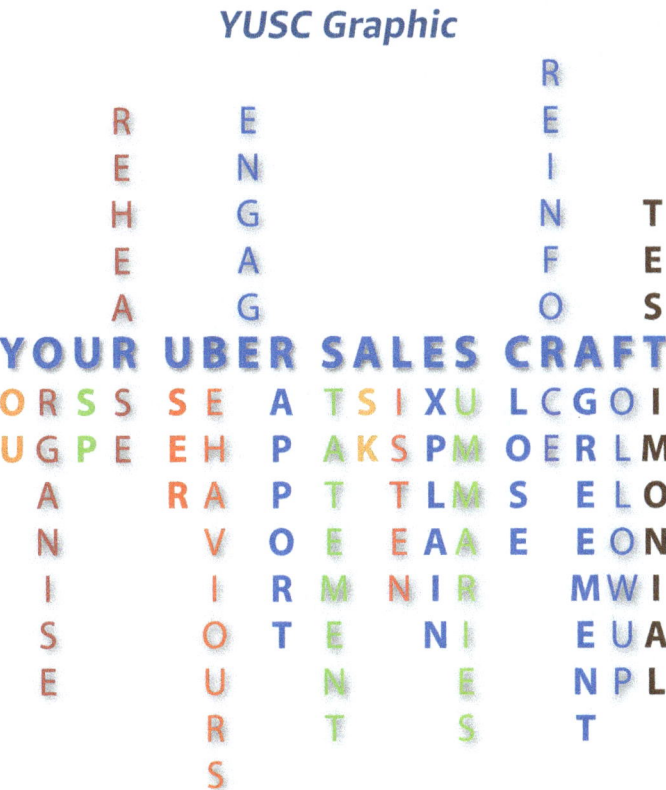

As you can see **YOURUBERSALESCRAFT** is created from useful steps that need to be concidered along the way for your sales process and for your preperation.

**YOUR UBER** is mainly concerned with your preperation, targeting and planning, pre call if you like.

**SALES CRAFT** is more related to incall and post sale activities.

# YOU

*'It's a real problem, when products don't sell themselves!' Brian Gwyther*

No matter how great a product is, or how much your customer needs your service, salespeople need to be mentally prepared. Not just for sales calls, customer interactions, planning and value propositions, but equally important, is the need for you to prepare **yourself.**

## Build on your weak areas!

It's important if we want to improve ourselves, we need to strengthen where we are weakest. Our strengths will always hold up and you will develop them more easily than where we are weak. So we need to understand our weaknesses in better detail. What do you feel confident in doing? Where don't you? Where are you weakest? What areas do you need to develop? Are you comfortable speaking to a group? Are you a confident person? Where do you excel? What do you enjoy? Do you fully understand the product or service? Am I in the right frame of mind?

There are many questions here and we need to be honest with ourselves, with honest answers. Once we realise a problem – as with life – we can deal with it. It's a case of addressing your weakness – uncovering it – seeing it - and know that there is a way to address it. Levelling up on our weaknesses can take many forms – re-training – taking a different attitude – seeking family or colleague support – research online or books – doing a skydive to raise money to gain confidence – like I say, many forms. Some of you may be doing this right now by reading this, if so – Great! - because you've taken you first steps in becoming more successful in what you want to achieve!

Never be afraid to ask for help. Period! It is essential to your success that you understand where your weaknesses are and address them. If you're with a firm that gives annual appraisals then ensure you get the support to develop, go on that Excel course or Presentation course, take more time to make less errors in a proposal or bid, sort out your speling!, read through emails before you send them to ensure accuracy, go on that negotiation course, badger your boss to set up the SPIN training.

If I give you a sporting analogy:

*'If you want to play better, play with better players'.*

Good, professional colleagues will encourage and bring your game on. We instinctively know this, if you work with people who are unprofessional, don't care, do the minimum – well, that's what you'll learn! If this is your situation then – how will you grow and develop?

Remember - honest answers!

Always reach out to colleagues or your manager for clarity and answers. Gain clarity of how they addressed a challenge or situation.

*I worked with a colleague who was having great success in gaining product compliance in her territory and when discussing her success, I found out she was dealing with a subset of customer that many of us, including me, didn't engage with. Remember the NHS is complex! This message soon went through the company that these people (Pharmacy Optimisation technicians) were a vital contact we needed engagement with.*

I would always encourage 'town halls' within a sales meeting where we share experiences of best practice and new ways to be effective or even reinforcing what you are doing is the correct way. Feed information and success' into 'Good News Friday' emails to the company.

Over time, you read books; attend courses, even watching YouTube will give an insight into how you can develop your craft. The worst thing you can do is know you can be better and not take action!

*You may need to 'force' yourself into a situation – for instance, going 'first' in a role-play is one situation many people don't enjoy. Rather than letting the stress build up and build up as you inevitably know it's your turn soon. Be brave, and get it 'over with', by doing so you are, in fact, facing your fear – head on – and winning!*

*If you're not so good at presenting PowerPoint in front of customers have a colleague or manager co-present with you to help build confidence. Try to copy their style (if it's good!). Find a way and suggest a solution that could work for you and reach out for support.*

Successful salespeople must also be mentally prepared to:

- experience failure
- learn from their failures
- move on to the next opportunity

Success is not a given and you cannot 'win them all' but with practice your success rate will outstrip your failure rate and that is how we are successful.

*I once had a project for £75,000 shelved because the Hospital, through financial issues (via government funding) postponed the project for the following financial year even though, value, savings and efficiencies were proven. Like I say you can't win them all and sometimes things are outside of your power of influence. Recognise it, and keep the opportunity for the sale open for another time when it can be closed. Also don't be fooled by super sales people who win everything – they don't!☺ I've taken business from them and so will you☺*

## Stress

Stress is usually a reaction to mental or emotional pressure. It's often related to feeling like you're losing control over something, but sometimes there's no obvious cause. When you're feeling anxious or scared, your body releases stress hormones such as adrenaline and cortisol. We all suffer from stress and this can come at us from many directions but we'll discuss a few ways to manage it.

Some common stress point:

Anxiety – some sort of pressure from life, a situation.

Fear of failure – being unsure of your action, low confidence in yourself.

Life pressures - can easily overwhelm us.

We know we are stressed sometimes, we can feel it. Some of the common signs are:

>Irritable, aggressive, impatient or wound up
>Over-burdened
>Anxious, nervous or afraid
>Like your thoughts are racing and you can't switch off
>Unable to enjoy yourself
>Depressed
>Uninterested in life
>Like you've lost your sense of humour
>A sense of dread
>Worried about your health
>Neglected or lonely.

In order to challenge our stress, we want to change from a stress state to a more relaxed state. So, if we want a new result, we need a new action.

*In order to loss our negative emotional state we need to <u>change our behaviours</u>, to change our emotional state.*

So below are a few tips to that may help with managing stress.

Change the way we use our physiology (physical body):

Posture - Don't Slump
Head up - not down
Talk more slowly - not too fast
Breath full and deep – not shallow
Shoulders back – open and confident

Adopting these 'power positions', you'll be 33% more likely to take 'action' that you wouldn't have before. These help create more certainty within yourself

Change your focus by asking yourself better questions:

What are you proud of? Focus on that pride moment – How do you feel?
What are you grateful for? Focus on this
What's your best achievement? Focus on this
What are you excited for? Focus on this

Take breaks! During you working day it's important to take breaks to allow you mind some recuperation time and to relax. If you're working from home, go for a walk, take the dog out. If you're on the road take time to stop and eat lunch, have a coffee. You'll come back to you work refreshed and in a better mind set! If you are suffering from stress you should also talk with your doctor and seek some further help.

## Sabotage stress

Whilst stress does come in many forms, I'd like to address one that I've had some experience of and I'll call it Sabotage Stress. It's the kind of stress that, with hindsight, you may recognise. It's the stress you put on yourself – often because you believe 'stuff you're doing' is warranted. Most of the time, it is not. It is rarely necessary to work late, not read to kids in bed or work over the weekend.

Also what needs to be realised is, what you are working on? Is it 'extra' work that really is not necessary and won't 'actually' make a difference to an outcome? Only you can answer this for your workload. And lastly, you have the right to say 'no'. Resist taking on work that someone else should have completed, or is not needed, realise your worth and take control, you have your own job to do and your own work/life balance to maintain.

## Passion

Sometimes a life/career change is what is needed in order you to realise your full potential. Passion is a multiplier for sales success so ensure you are employed in a sector that you enjoy and are passionate about. Most managers faced at interview with a sales person with skill and another with passion: will choose passion every time – you can teach skill – it's far harder to teach passion! But it's not just that, passion is infectious!

*I worked with a self-employed consultant who had developed his own system for managing waste in the NHS and watching his passion for how the system would address the needs of the customer was totally infectious. You could see the clients respond to this and give their buy-in more easily, and he was a good sales person!*

I hope you have people around you with a passion for their job and that's the environment we should be working in to develop ourselves. Passion can also be described as Personal Motivation and so it's vital to your sales success to be personally motivated with a passion around what you sell.

## ORGANISE

*"For every minute spent organizing, an hour is earned."* Benjamin Franklin

Organising your day can often result in the difference between achieving the task you need for a customer sale or having to constantly put off important tasks and so delaying or even losing a sale. If you use your time with an organised and strategic approach, you're more likely to be the most productive you've ever been.

'One of my team had literally got themselves quite worked up and confused over planning their strategy and admin and I was so pleased they reached out to me for some help. So we discussed the situation, broke the tasks into manageable pieces, binned the things they didn't need to worry about and created a list of tasks, there were 7. This way, there was clarity and the discussion helped to alleviate the pressure that had been built up in their mind.'

Organization is, commonly, one of the most challenging activities for field sales people to completely achieve and implement. With the number of things that need to be done on a day to day basis, field salespeople have numerous things competing for their attention.

Organising yourself is vital to achieve the clarity you need to achieve a given outcome and I'll split this into 3 sections that I think are critical at this stage: Admin, Prioritising and Planning.

## Admin

There's a number of comments around doing Administration I've heard over time, 'I don't do admin' 'too busy selling' 'I hate admin'. Getting sales people to organize and manage their days or filling in call reports, can stop teams and people from reaching the goals they have set. But interestingly there is a flip side; some sales people spend more of their time on administrative tasks than they have actually selling. Often planning and making lists and trying to understand customers can lead to a vicious circle that can literally stop them doing anything else.

In order to free up time, you need to place a focus on eliminating the tasks you shouldn't be doing (as discussed in the previous chapter) as well as the ones you should. The main reason for this is the countless number of activities that simply waste time each day without contributing to helping achieve sales targets or goals.

Time management in sales comes down to how you'll prioritize and maximize your time each day. Instead of working more hours, which takes you away from your personal life, a few easy-to-use organizational tips can drastically improve your efficiency.

## Tips to Help You Stay Organised

### 1. Administrative Tasks

Admin tasks are the #1 thing that prevents us from spending more time in the field, where you should be right! Feeling less stressed by the number of things weighing on us is a good thing!

This will allow us to divert more of our energy and attention away from unnecessary tasks, and focus on things that will move a sale through the process.

To-do Lists are GREAT! So make a list of the things you need to do that day and or week etc. Use tasks in Outlook or Salesforce or some app, I use a notebook and so long as you're getting organised it's a win!

**Prioritise them!** What's the most important job on the list? A job may not be so 'Important', but it carries a time pressure, so this goes up the list, either way, get yourself organised. If tasks are on your list that are not your job/responsibility then push them back to those who can manage them. You can prioritise many things, more on this later.

## 2. CRM

CRM stands for "Customer Relationship Management" and can be incredibly useful to log your calls and activity/emails but also to create opportunity pipelines to track where you are in a sales process. We won't be going into detail here but if you have access to one ensure you use it and understand its benefits to keep you organised and on track.

## 3. Procrastination

'Procrastination is the act of delaying or postponing a task or set of tasks. So, whether you refer to it as procrastination or something else, it is the force that prevents you from following through on what you set out to do'

Procrastination is a behaviour often seen just before certain times of the month. It often shows itself before tasks such as Expenses, Reports, and Updating CRM. Schedule yourself the time in your diary and stop procrastinating and just do it – you'll be surprised how much easier the task is than the actual build up to it in your mind.

## 4. Manage Your Inbox

Like most people, your inbox is full up and seemingly doesn't stop.

It would be great if we could get people to start a protocol of not copying in unnecessary people to their email wouldn't it! Maybe you could suggest it to the bosses? However for now, you could start by blocking off time in your calendar each day to read and respond to emails to give you time to complete you important tasks. I often use the flags in Outlook to remind me of what need addressing today /tomorrow etc so if you haven't looked at this then try it. Remember that to be organised, we need to also allocate time to be organised. Eliminate all distractions during this time to complete the task as efficiently and effectively as possible.

*You could set an out of office for the times you are reviewing your emails and tasks to help with reducing distraction. Tim Ferriss from The 4-Hour Work Week created a pretty witty template you could use:*

*"Due to high workload, I am currently checking and responding to email twice daily at 12:00pm and 4:00pm.*

*If you require urgent assistance (please ensure it is urgent) that cannot wait until either 12:00pm or 4:00pm, please contact me via phone at ----------."*

## 5. Eliminate Distractions

It's hard to focus when your favourite YouTube channel is just a click away! To ensure you stay focused, ruthlessly get rid of every distraction. Don't have personal web info on you work computer, work is for work. Put your mobile phones out of sight. It's all too tempting to check social media or your texts if you can see or hear notifications come up.

## Conclusion

The goal isto work smarter as opposed to harder. Nobody wants to work longer hours to make the same money or just achieve minimal bonus/commission. By eliminating distractions and having a strategic, focused approach, you're going to spend more time doing the things that will actually lead to great sales.

## Prioritise

## What is Prioritisation?

Prioritisation is imperative in your understanding of your accounts as it is the biggest determining factor of your sales success. It can be tricky and a difficult task in your sales planning, but if done well, it can dramatically help you reach your target or goal. It clears shows which accounts to target your time and actions on.

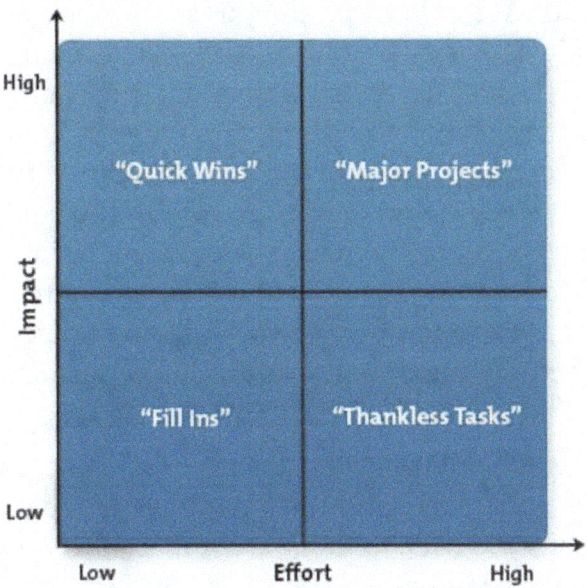

You may have seen the picture above before and it's very intuitive.

Effort – It's easier to sell to existing customers than new ones where there is no relationship, focus on these first where possible. However if you need larger growth you may well need to target new customers and set actions in motion to start a new relationship.

Impact – How will the account/customer impact your sales figures? The higher the impact the more valuable they are as an account to prioritise to approach for a sale.

This is an easy chart to draw up yourself and grab a coffee then plot out your accounts. You also may find you're spending a lot of time and effort in accounts that aren't actually of value to your business and your success.

**3 useful ways for effective account prioritisation:**

**1.** The existing sales of the account: No matter if it's existing business or potential game changing new account, if the account is large then; invest your time, efforts and money to nurture it. Large accounts fall into either 'Quick wins' or 'Major Project'. Either way, keep them informed of your product or service, meet them at exhibitions/trade shows or seminars, and ask them to consult on a project or seek their expertise. Keep updating them about your company's success; gain an advocacy from the Key Opinion Leader by asking for testimonials or case studies. You need to apply your knowledge of your industry and think 'out of the box' so you can make a difference. So, now you have prioritized the large accounts, but also started planning for success with them. Additionally, this type of activity will empower you to save 'At-risk' large accounts. This type of activity needs to be a habit in the account prioritization process.

**2.** Determining the potential sales of a new account: This account prioritization metric, determining potential sales, takes a bit more work. To do this, you need to follow a comparison type of method. Here, you need to compare current sales and size of one of your customer to the target accounts size in order to extrapolate the potential sales. Next, identify products you could be selling to them but currently aren't. This can be done through face-to-face interviews with the customer by the salespeople. Often though you can work this out from reviewing your current sales data – find the GAPs – and there's your target products with an approximate value based on other customers of similar sizes.

**3.** Reduce your time in the 'Fill Ins and Thankless Task' accounts. Your time is valuable and it is important you realise that you may be wasting it. It's worth bearing in mind though that there still needs to be a relationship kept with these 'low impact - high effort' accounts as a competitor may slip up, the buyer retires or something changes and… You're in! But you need to either back off with the time you spend here or get more 'smart' with them. By getting 'smart' I mean bring them to a conclusion. If they keep asking things or tasks of you and are not buying more as a result., it's OK to say 'No' to a customer. One way is to use the 'Higher Power' tact – 'My boss won't authorise this anymore as X or Y needs to happen first'. Your time is valuable as is the need for a customer to work with you, if it's only one way then there's no 'win win'. There are some personality types who like people standing up to them and offering a robust conversation, who will give you respect for this, rather than bending to their every whim. Sometimes it can be useful to behave according to their personality type. We'll talk about personality types later on.

**GAP Analysis**
Gap analysis involves the comparison of actual performance with potential or desired performance. So in order to keep it simple – you sell currently £80,000 pa and the target is £100,000, the gap is £20,000. And so you spend your time investigating how to achieve £20k of growth, on the assumption that the £80k continues. This is easier than working on a £100k sales plan (also don't assume anything as it makes an ASS of U and ME!)
With the GAP now identified you can describe what that looks like – services not being used, Product range not being utilised in some areas etc. You may need some help to understand a product offering to gain confidence in selling it. Whatever the GAP is identify it and write out your remedial actions to address it.

Here's is a basic overview of a first stage GAP analysis to help get your mind in order to then develop a more detailed sales plan

| Objective | Gap Description | Remedial Action |
|---|---|---|
| To Increase Annual Sales | Lack of sales direction, Lack of knowledge, Current customer base limited | Prioritisation of accounts, Review Top 20 for GAP's in product use, Segmentation of accounts by product, Create a target list with strategy for each account, Increase Product knowledge for target products. |
| **Current state** | | |
| £2,000,000 | | |
| **Desired State** | | |
| £2,500,000 | | |
| **Gap Identified** | | |
| £500,000 | | |

In all my time in sales, I've rarely needed more than this principle so let's keep it simple.

## Account Segmentation

There's a good reason that account segmentation works well. It shows us a way of further prioritising your customers to best match activity and/or objectives to the right customer base. You can categorise your accounts into all manner of segments and there are a few I will discuss briefly but as you get the idea, you will see that segmentation possibilities are almost endless.

### First are Products or Service

Now, in the prioritise section, we discussed looking at high spend 'Major Project' accounts, however, because of a specific sales product campaign; this target account may not apply. We are being very specific now – by targeting sales potential of a certain product into a certain account and so our list of priority accounts will look different. Your top account may not have a need for the product you are targeting, so you may be dealing with your 4th overall account but it's the top one for product X. It's important you can look at your account with this type of analytical mind to truly understand where to best focus your activity.

### Second are Competitor accounts

If you can get your hands on competitor sales data you'll be able to see which accounts your competitor is working in and from this, decide a suitable approach to the account in order to affect a change in their buying habits. You can use local knowledge, other reps information, online info, magazine, who's connected to who on LinkedIn to gain valuable information on a potential target account.

**Third are Relationships** – as a broad description, these are the account relationships where:

1. You have a great relationship,
2. Ones when you have to improve them
3. And those where you hardly know them.

And each of these customer relationships could be scored out of 10.

Cool 1-3 =unknown to us or only one call so early days.

Warm is ranked 4-5= still fact finding and we will have met them a few times.

Hot is ranked 6-7 = positivity and asking for quotes or trialling a product or something similar.

Advocate is ranked 8-10 = they buy and could advocate for us (10).

For instance, you may score a relationship as 7 – often because you're a great salesperson, and like everyone, so you need to be honest and not over score relationships! You may get on with say the Head of Purchasing well but you may not have a great relationship with the merchandising manager or Finance manager. Recognising this allows you to start planning to get to know these other people in the account better.

*In my recent Regional Business Manager role, we set up this segmentation task for the sales team to rate their relationships with the key customer contacts. It was interesting to see how many 10's there were with our Key customers but not so high a rating in the others. This is not a criticism, but informed us that we need to do more with the relationship in other areas to augment the sales we wanted in a new customer base. But it also highlighted that we focus too much on one customer type within the business and needed to bring that focus to other customer teams and other speciality nurses to.*

Working with the 6-7 customers, we need to develop them up.

And getting those introductions for the 1&2's to push them up a level is important for your long term business relationships 2-5 years from now. Also lever those '10' relationship to help sales in other areas or with other customers by supporting you and being an advocate for your business.

**A fourth way** of segmenting accounts is how well an account/customer is engaging with us within the buying cycle (PEAK).

## PEAK

I've used the **PEAK** system for this cutomer engagement stage. Use it to map where a customer is in the buying cycle with you. I look at it from a sales person's point of view with our interactions with that customer.

Peak stands for: Prospect, Engage, Acquire, Keep

Prospect is they may be unknown to us or have just sent an enquiry to our company

Engage is we will have met them a few times and they are engaging with us.

Acquire means they are asking for quotes or trialling a product or something similar.

Keep is a buying customer and may advocate for us.

If you have a number of Engagers, you need to ensure you get them across the line to become Acquirers and the Keepers. you need to figure out what will push the customer to the next stage, What do they need? What will move them to action?

# YOUR UBER SALES CRAFT

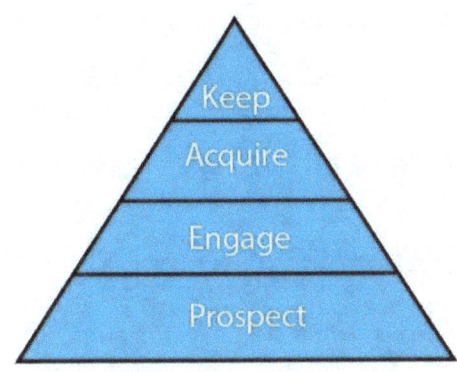

In PEAK, the system looks like a triangle

With all the Prospects at the bottom, we work with them, support and sell them on through to the Keep section where they are customers. The more Prospects we have, with your better skill set, then the more we can bring to the Keep stage and achieve our sales revenues.

*When I worked in capital sales, I needed to have at least 3 times the number of potential sales coming through in order to achieve target because of unforeseen issues or delays. And yes LOL you could say I wasn't very good at sales☺, but you'd be wrong! Throughout the companies and the sectors I've been in, if you had a target of say £100,000 you would need to be prospecting and engaging at least £300,000 to achieve target. The filling of the pipeline is vital for sales and this is a role where Marketing should be by your side helping you get fresh leads to follow up. If they aren't, then engage with them to discuss options like: Mailers, Advertising, Exhibitions, Marketing/Sales articles in trade magazines and testimonial papers you can use. Get your thinking cap on and push your colleagues to help you sell.*

## SWOT Analysis

A SWOT analysis is a strategic planning technique used to help you identify strengths, weaknesses, opportunities, and threats related to business, competition or planning.

They are dead easy to create and here's a simple example

| Strengths | Weakness |
|---|---|
| Opportunities | Threats |

Just fill in the boxes regarding the account or product (or whatever the project or plan is) to bring to the fore, in your mind, what the SWOT's are and so you can start to formulate how to use them or overcome them.

## Planning

To this point we've given a lot of thought to ourselves, our customers, what we're looking to sell and to whom; and this is the basis of your sales plan. But in order to produce a good plan we need to put this into some sort of order so:

Use sales data from the previous year and search for trends.

Use a GAP analysis to uncover what needs to grow to achieve your targets.

Start sales forecasting based on demand trends and historical data.

Use the Account Segmentation and prioritisation information to list target accounts.

We could plot how engaged they are with the PEAK system.

Clarify your objectives and create sales target accounts that meet your revenue goals.

Assess your current situation, including weaknesses that will act as stoppers and strengths that will help. (A SWOT analysis)

Determine the parameters used to measure your success.

Create new initiatives based on opportunities you may have passed on in previous years.

Involve stakeholders from departments that can help your outcomes such as Marketing.

Outline actions or tasks using SMART goals/objectives and GANT charts where necessary to help plan activity timeframes.

Bear in mind that once you start developing your plan, it should be treated like a 'living document' and should be revisited and adjusted when necessary.

When you select an account to target and in discussions with the customer, there's an issue that cannot be overcome, you should feel OK to drop it from the plan and put the reserve choice in. Otherwise you'll be banging your head against a brick wall to sell to an account that clearly isn't ready yet to be sold to. It's at this point that some will say 'Well you haven't done a good enough job with the customer to sell to them'. Yep, we've all had those managers! There's a 'yes' and 'no' to this as it's dependant on the situation and reason for not moving together with you. But either way, in the real world, with people who are doing the job, it's best to not be negative about what happened and always be supportive. Sometime the best skill is to know when to walk away, keeping your relationship intact and your company's reputation with the customer to return another day. Remember that we need 3 times the Prospects in order to reach the close (Keep) so this will happen to us all, we just need to show we tried to mitigate against loss of sales Prospects.

**SMART goals**

SMART goals are a fairly new idea. In 1981, George T. Doran, a consultant and former director of corporate planning for Washington Water Power Company, published a paper called, "There's a SMART Way to Write Management's Goals and Objectives." He introduces SMART goals as a tool to create criteria to help improve the chances of success in accomplishing a goal.

You are more likely to achieve them, driving your sale forward through the process if you have SMART in mind.

SMART in more detail:

### S – Specific

When setting a goal, be specific about what it is you want to accomplish. This is the main aspect of your goal. This isn't a detailed list of how you're going to achieve the goal, but you should be answering 6 of the 'W' questions.

Who – Consider who needs to be involved to achieve the goal (this is especially important when you're working on a group project).
What – What you are trying to accomplish and don't be afraid to get very detailed.
When – You'll get more specific about this question under the "timely" section of defining SMART goals, but you should at least set a time frame.
Where – This question may not always apply, especially if you're setting personal goals, but if there's a location or relevant event, specify it here.
Which – Determine any related obstacles or requirements. This question can be beneficial in deciding if your goal is realistic.
Why – What is the reason for the goal? When it comes to using this method for sales, the answer will likely be along the lines of target achievement.

### M – Measurable

What metrics are you going to use to determine if you meet the goal? This makes a goal more perceptible because it provides a way to measure progress. If it's a project that's going to take a few months to complete, then set some milestones by considering specific tasks to accomplish.

**A – Achievable**

This stresses on how important a goal is to you and what you can do to make it possible and may require developing new skills and changing attitudes. The goal is meant to inspire motivation, not discouragement. Think about how to accomplish the goal and if you have the tools/skills needed. If you don't currently possess those skills, consider what it would take for you to achieve them.

**R – Realistic or Relevant**

Realistic is focusing on something that makes sense with your wider business goals. For example, if the goal is to launch a new product, it should be something that is in alignment with your overall business objectives. You may be looking to launch a new product, but if your company is not working in the target market then the goal wouldn't be relevant.

**T – Timely**

Anyone can set goals, but if it lacks realistic timing, chances are you're not going to succeed. Providing a target date for your goal is important. Ask specific questions about the goal deadline and what can be accomplished within that time period. If the goal will take three months to complete, it's useful to define what should be achieved half-way through the process. Providing time constraints can also create a sense of urgency and so will help you prioritise goals.

## USP

*"The best USP you can offer is you" Brian Gwyther*

Wikipedia says: 'In marketing, the unique selling proposition (USP), also called the unique selling point, or the unique value proposition (UVP) in the business model canvas, is the marketing strategy of informing customers about how one's own brand or product is superior to its competitors (in addition to its other values). It was used in successful advertising campaigns of the early 1940s. The term was coined by television advertising pioneer Rosser Reeves of Ted Bates & Company.

Definition:

A unique selling proposition (USP) refers to the unique benefit exhibited by a company, service, product or brand that enables it to stand out from competitors. The unique selling proposition must be a feature that highlights product benefits that are meaningful to consumers. USP focuses on explicit claims of uniqueness involving an objectively verifiable product attribute or benefit-in-use.

**What is your USP?** Your unique selling point. I often relate this to a few specific things but firstly: YOU are a USP! Your passion, your organisational skill, your commitment to the customer and their business needs. A unique selling proposition more traditionally is the one thing that makes your business stand out from the competition. It's a specific benefit that makes your business offering or product stand out when compared to your competitors in your market. Forming a factual USP helps focus your marketing strategy and influences messaging, branding, copywriting, and other marketing decisions. At its core, a USP should quickly answer a potential customer's first question when they encounter you or your brand, and should be in any 'elevator pitch' you develop.

Upon first meeting you, a customer will be thinking "What makes you different from my current supplier?"

Your USP plays to your strengths and should be based on what makes your brand or product unique and therefore valuable to your customers. Being "unique" is rarely a strong USP in itself. You have to differentiate around some aspect your customer cares about; otherwise your messaging won't be as effective as it could be.

A compelling USP should be: Confident, but defendable: A specific position thatencourages you to make a case against competing products is more memorable than a basic stance, like "we sell high quality products." Focus on what your customer might value. "Unique" won't count for much if it's not something your customer holds any value in. More than a slogan: While a slogan is one way your USP can be communicated, it's also something that you can embody in other areas of your business, from your environmental policy to your supply chain. You should be able to talk the talk and walk the walk.

**Vistaprint's** Unique Selling Proposition: *Fast, Cheap Printing for*

*Growing Businesses on a Budget*

**Saddleback Leather's** Unique Selling Proposition: *Rugged Leather Goods with a 100-Year Warranty*

**FedEx Corporation** Unique Selling point: *"When it absolutely, positively has to be there overnight."*

Now as I imagine many of you work for companies that already have a USP then, do you know it? As previously stated the USP should be within your elevator pitch, do you have an elevator pitch? If not then let's look at this a little further.

## Elevator Pitch

How to write your own unique selling proposition

Now that we've looked at some examples of strong USPs from other businesses, you might be wondering how you can go about creating, uncovering, or refining your own elevator pitch. Every USP is going to be unique! But there is a process to creating one into an elevator pitch. Here's how you can write yours if there isn't one in place for you right now.

Make a list of all the potential differentiators of your product/brand and what you sell, get specific. Compelling marketing messages rely on precision: they solve the exact right problem and communicate that benefit to customers in their own words. Research the competition. Who are your competitors and what are their USPs? Look for gaps where you can potentially introduce your brand differently. Products in the same category can be positioned in wildly different ways—Coats, for example, can emphasize style, comfort, or durability.

Compare your most unique benefits against your customer's needs. Are there any customer needs that haven't been filled? Do you see any pain points that you can sell to that your competitors haven't? Compile the data. Take the information that you've learned, and sort through it to pick out your strongest USP for use in your pitch.

Think about viable ways to apply it across your business. Applied properly, a USP can be woven into different areas of your business, from your brand name to your return policy to reinforce the idea to your customers

Let's see how this works, using a pet clothing equipment supply business as an example. Note that everything in brackets can be changed to suit the specifics of your company, and that this framework can apply to both companies and individual products.

For [pet lovers]

Who [need premium customised pet clothing]

[Pet Cloth]

Is [the world's only dedicated bespoke pet clothing service]

That [provides a pet fitting service,].

Unlike [other pet supply companies],

[Pet Cloth Emporium] is [the only pet clothing & customisation service in the UK that caters specifically for pets].

I think you get the picture☺ so go write your own USP and create your elevator pitch.

## Pareto Law

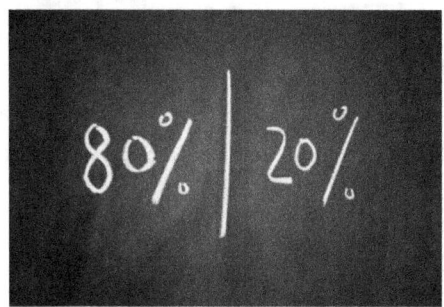

Pareto's Law takes its name from the Italian economist Vilfredo Pareto. He noticed that 80% of Italy's land and wealth was owned by 20% of the population. Pareto's Law put into practise in a sales environment; we believe that 80% of a company's sales will come from 20% of its company's customers. The Pareto Principle is also known as the Pareto Rule or Law or the 80/20 Rule. You may have been applying Pareto to your business without knowing it. Why do we list the Top 20 accounts? Because these accounts are the ones creating your sales and so they need to be managed, grown and maintained.

And so this is true for you, 80% of your sales will likely come for 20% of you customers. If this is the case then I would always encourage building up that 80%. Like having all your eggs in one basket, you are at risk of a disaster if one of those 20% accounts switches to a competitor. You need to plan for looking after the 20% but also increase your customer base so you are less at risk. We lose customers – Fact. And sometimes there is nothing we can do to stop it. Sales are not black and white, and the more we can do to mitigate against losses has to be a benefit.

This Pareto principle also serves as a general reminder that the relationship between inputs and outputs is not balanced and often a 20% cause will create an 80% effect. If you're specific in what you plan & target then this will lead to greater result for you, winning that game changer account moves you from 80/20 to 70/30 – GREAT!

## Company Values

As sales people, we need to act in a professional way and often work via the company values. So if you work for a company, do you know what they are? There maybe words such as, Integrity, Honest, Responsible, Innovative. You will be expected to act accordingly to them.

Companies will also have a value statement. The term "value statement" is simple. It's a statement which conveys the values and priorities of the company or organization it represents. This lets your customers and employees know what's important to your business and the kind of culture it has created.

The performance value statement from Adidas is 'Sport is the foundation for all we do and executional excellence is a core value of our Group.'

IKEA's value statement, 'At IKEA, our vision is to create a better everyday life for the many people.'

If you have company values and a value statement, then act by it and try to live up to it.

## Value Added service

A value-added service (VAS) may well have originated in the telecommunications industry, and is a term for non-core services, or, in short, all services beyond standard voice calls and fax transmissions. However, it can be used in any service industry, for services available at little or no cost, to promote their primary business.

This is a differentiator similar in aspect to the USP. It describes the extra service that is above and beyond the purchase of the product, basically at no cost, and that you offer more value than either the incumbent or a competitor.

So if we take an example of my current healthcare industry, we sell barrier products, yes, but we also sell the VAS on top and this takes the form of education and upskilling staff in its use. We also create educational 'Pathways' bespoke to the Hospital for the products use, we allow access to eLearning free, perform ward audits and our own company nurse will hold training days and education to augment the work the hospital already does. But not only that, we offer online downloadable toolkits, and patient information, I could go on, but if you think my customer is buying our barrier cream, think again, they are buying our whole service offering, and me to support them.

So ensure you fully understand what you are offering and make sure you are stating this. You need to create your proposition to include the VAS as more often than not these days; it's the service/VAS element that will win your deals.

We've been using the 'Rule of 3' in order to articulate our value added service and this has developed into what we call our 'Value Proposition'. Its widely know now that 3 is a good number that lands well with customers and so this supports the Value Proposition.

*So currently my company has developed a Value proposition and there are 3 arms or pillars to it: Digital – Clinical - Economics. And we created brochures, PowerPoint presentations and structure our sales pitches to include these when discussing these with our customers. It lands well with customer and they react well to our offering because it's targeted to their pain points.*

The Value Added Services/Value Propositions, are developed from a customer needs perspective. So within your industry there will be common customer needs that can help shape your VAS and so it's important you understand their needs and research it if necessary. We also use industry 'Buzz words' to help talk the same language as our customer – speaking directly to them. Which is why 'Economics' was used in the proposition; this speaks directly to the pressures of the NHS in the UK for clinical outcomes/cost and their budgets.

Depending on your service and product purchase route theres another interesting way to highlight this VAS to your customer. There's a little more on values in the USER chapter.

## Sales Strategies
Your selling strategies will differ, depending on the type of customer, your relationship and where they want to move towards. That said, there are essentially four main selling strategies:

> Script-based selling, Needs-satisfaction selling, Consultative selling, and Strategic partnering.

We'll take a look at each of these in turn but often there is a need to be flexible and adaptable to be able to switch your strategy dependant on the situation, customer or process you're in.

## Script-Based Selling
Salespeople will have to remember or read a script-based selling strategy. Script-based selling is also called canned selling. The term "canned" comes from the fact that the sales pitch is "straight out of a can", or standardized. Back in the late 1880s, companies

began to use professional salespeople to distribute their products. Companies like National Cash Register (NCR) realized that some salespeople were far more effective than others, so they brought those salespeople into the head office and had them give their sales pitches. A stenographer wrote each pitch down, and then NCR's sales managers knitted the pitches into one effective script. In 1894, the company started one of the world's first sales schools, which taught people to sell using the types of scripts developed by NCR.

Script-based selling works well when the needs of customers don't vary much. Even if they do, a script can provide a salesperson with a polished and professional description of how an offering meets each of their needs. The salesperson will ask the customer a few questions to uncover his or her need, and then provides the details that meet it as written in the script. Scripts will also ensure that the salesperson includes all the important details about a product.

## Needs-Satisfaction Selling

This is the process of asking questions to identify your customer problems and needs and then tailoring a sales response to match and answer those needs. This is called needs-satisfaction selling. This form of selling works best if the needs of customers vary but the products being offered are fairly standard. You ask 'open' questions to understand the needs then present a solution. This method of selling was popularized by Neil Rackham, who further developed the SPIN selling approach. SPIN stands for situation questions, problem questions, implications, and needs-payoff, four types of questions that are designed to fully understand how a problem is creating a need. More on SPIN later in the book

Need satisfaction will be where we spend a lot of our time especially when we are first getting to know our customer. We need to ask questions to uncover their issues, pain points, needs etc.

## Consultative Selling

You may think needs-satisfaction selling and consultative selling seem the same. But they aren't, for the consultative sell the sales person will be highly skilled in a subject and is able to vary the product or service offering dependant on the needs of the customer. Often these sales can take years in order to work through to an agreed resolution. That said, we can also work at a consultative level with our customers if you are the expert and the customer needs your help to address a problem they have. I often think there's a subtle modification of language here. We are specifically selling to the problem - and not selling a product. We aren't matching a need with an immediate benefit of your product; we're guiding them through a problem scenario, where the outcome leads to them leaning on our expertise, consultation, advice and product/service offering in a customised or revised form.

*My colleague and I were called in to a new medical unit that was being opened by a manager who oversaw the project (and was let down by a competitor) but he didn't know the waste management side of the project. The Legal state, the waste management regulations, types of waste and transportation law. We did, and we consulted them through the process and with specific proposals and actions to enable the opening of the unit on time. None of this sale was feature and benefit based.*

If you have a good Value Added Service that goes along side your products, you should be able to achieve the consultative sell approach and address the problem of a customer with a customised VAS backed up with the product offering – if you can try it – be a consultant!

## Strategic-Partner Selling

When the quality of the relationship between the buyer and seller moves toward a strategic partnership, the selling strategy gets more involved than even consultative selling. In strategic-partner selling, both parties invest resources and share their expertise with each other to create solutions that jointly grow one another's businesses. You will develop Key Opinion Leaders; for example, who may invest in your company, and position themselves as a strategic partner to the colleagues he works with. They will try to become a trusted partner in the business you are involved in.

*I once worked with a Neuro-Radiology professor who having bought shares in the company and helped develop the treatment I was selling. He opened many doors for us as that Strategic Partner and sales in the UK rose very nicely. It was one of my roles to develop more strategic accounts in the UK and he was a KOL that helped achieve this.*

## Know Your Product

Having a strategy is nothing if you don't know your product inside out; you have to know what you're selling. If you don't know the features and benefits of the product or service you're selling, you won't be able to answer customer questions or handle objections. Ensure you are familiar with the products and services you sell by reading all marketing brochures, clinical papers, detail aids. You also need to understand thoroughly the Value added services or propositions that need to be developed and explained and often it is these that will win you the sales. You'll probably have to think on your feet in order to match the customer need to a suitable value proposition. Sometime you'll link a value proposition via a product feature/benefit. Organise these points in your mind and have clarity of what you're saying. Discuss this with colleagues and there's more on this in the Rehearse section of the system

## Show & Tell

Customers want to hear about the features and benefits of a product or service, but they're more impressed when they can see and touch the product or service, seeing it in action. If you can offer product samples, do it, while if you offer online tools to your customers, you could grant them trial access to the program. When customers can explore products or services, they can get a better idea of how it will fit it into their lives or business. This will also make the sales process run smoother. Try to be descriptive around how you talk about your product; don't just real off the benefits. Create a story or 'picture words'. Importantly, don't give the product over to them to early into their hands as, as soon as you do, you are no longer the focus. You must have achieved the uncovering of needs stage or the A.L.E in our YUORUBER**SALE**CRAFT SYSTEM first and have presented value propositions or at least Explained benefits in the **E** stage.

Any trial or demo of it in action should 'seal the deal' for you, so there is almost nothing left to say except, 'I'll buy that'. If you are in a trial situation for your product or service and it's vital you have agreed parameters and outcomes for the trial. You should also be pre-closing on this i.e. if 'X' can gain 75% acceptance by users and shows your processes are reduced by 20% then will you will be placing an order with us? I also like a less direct close such as 'if we meet the outcomes XX required, will you be recommending that we partner as your XX product supplier?' There are many ways to skin a cat and we'll discuss closing later in the C section of YUORUBERSALES**C**RAFT SYSTEM.

## Understand Your Target Customer

Customers have different needs and wants that make them gravitate toward specific products, services and companies. If you have knowledge of your target customers, you can readily identify their needs and help them find solutions. Each company has an ideal supplier it wants to partner with. Characteristics such a reputation, service, reliability, backup are all important for your customer and it's your role to help them see you can supply these reassurances. As such you need to know what you can offer and how to best match it to a customer as you discuss with them their situation and requirements. You can even discuss areas the customer may not have realised that your company's product can address. Don't always believe your customer is an expert in their field; they may be fresh into the job and need some guidance – of which you will be very useful to them.

## Get Referrals from Existing Customers

Existing customers can help gain you referrals and so it's important you ask for referrals or contacts that your product or service can help their colleague with. In turn this will help you maximise you sales potential and reach your targets. If your business model allows it, you could start a referral program that encourages your existing customers to suggest your business to their friends, so they can take advantage of discounts.

## Price Competitively

Pricing plays a major role in whether many consumers make a purchase, so it's important that part of your selling strategy includes pricing competitively. While you don't have to make your prices lower than or on par with your competitors, you should know their regular and sales prices for products and services. You may elect to price yours higher, but you must ensure that you can communicate the value in paying more for what you offer. Value-added benefits might include an extended warranty, service options, lifetime guarantees, and your level of expertise or the quality of your products.

Get the full picture

Don't always address price head on instead, get you customer to explain more about their situation. Ask, "Tell me more about X?" "Describe to issues this is having on Y?" This does a few of things: first, it allows you to get all the information out at once. By doing this you get a complete picture of what's really going on and can respond accordingly. And second, it gives you some time to think about how you want to respond. Our tendency is to jump in quickly, respond to the objection, and move on. But you need to take your time and get the prospect to talk more about it so you can get to the heart of the issue.

Don't introduce price too early in the conversation

Price objections often come when you give the price too soon. Before you talk about price in the call, you have to get the customer to see your value proposition and get them to realise the value of the solution. When you share the price too early in the conversation, you lose control. You move into the negotiation phase where all conversations going forward are going to focus around price instead of value and outcomes.

Focus on selling the value proposition

When you get a price objection, you haven't done a good enough job of selling the value. Go back to the customer's needs and goals.

Get them to restate what the solution is worth to them. When you get the prospect to see the value of the solution and you put it in financial terms, you'll get much less resistance on the price.

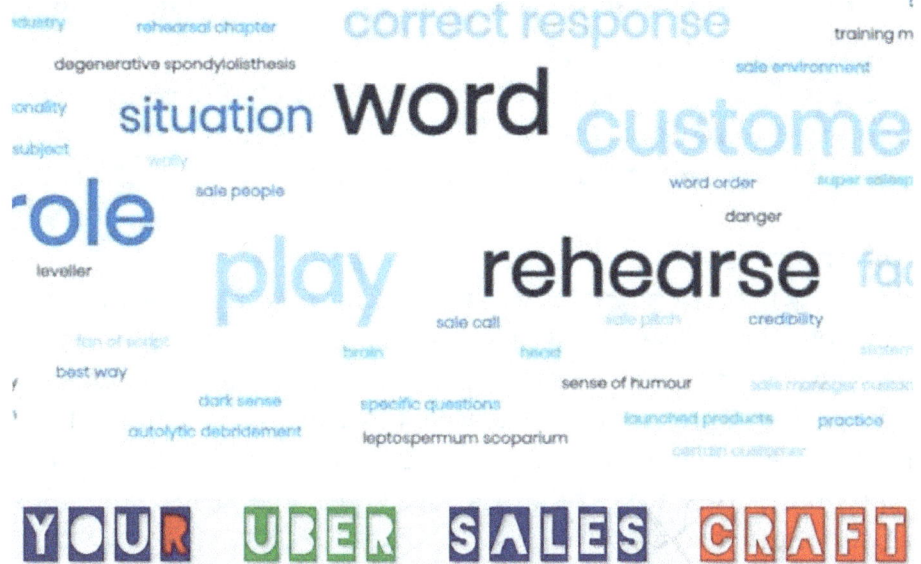

## REHEARSE

*"Won't it be great if I said we didn't need to do role-play!" Brian Gwyther*

One task that should be encouraged within a company and the sales people is to rehearse their sales pitch. I have never been a fan of scripts as you have a danger of sounding robotic and for our credibility; we should ensure our personality shows through. And so, ensure you can put the correct response into your own words and those that your customer will understand. As some of you know, we will talk differently to certain customers. That said you still need clarity of the correct response to a specific question or situation.

*To illustrate this rehearsal chapter, I had to start using words like: Autologous, autolytic debridement, Leptospermum scoparium, Degenerative spondylolisthesis with my sales calls. Yes, medical in the main and so I had to get familiar with them and not look like a Wally be-*

cause I didn't understand or couldn't say the words within my industry.

There is often a best way of describing a feature or benefit, so it's important to rehearse the words, rehearse the statement in your head, and also face to face within a 'safe' sales environment.

## Role-play

Role-play is often practiced at sales or training meetings. I know that role-play is the falsest of situations and that the 'Sales manager customer' never seems to act like one of your customers☺ but we need to realise this and accept it. Fighting it won't help. It does serve to help you get the correct 'word order' and therefore your brain into practice talking around the subject especially if it's a newly launched product.

Role-play also a leveller, as you remember those 'super salespeople'.... well it's interesting (and if you have a dark sense of humour like me, joyful!) to see them not perform as well as their mouth would have you believe, you may well realise that, if you even doubted yourself, you're not as bad as you thought!

For me the key has been to try and relax, I usually take a number of deep breaths whilst thinking of a personal situation that was stressful that I handled and overcame. We all have them so just pick yours and use it.

*For me, I use my black belt gradings in JKA karate where we had to do Kumite (the fighting) and in my early days, wore no pads on our hands. For me nothing was more stressful than having to fight someone who also wanted a black belt. And then, more fool me, I did it 4 more time to gain 4$^{th}$ Dan Black belt. So for me – doing a bit of role play, where someone wasn't trying to punch me in the face, doesn't seem so hard!*

Now that we have calmed you nerves – somewhat – keep it simple in role play because your mind will be racing and probably racing more that when you meet a 'real' customer. So, follow your basic sales process assuming that's the excercise:

1. Build rapport with general chit chat
2. Uncover Needs
3. Match those needs (with the 'script')
4. Close them in asking for the business
5. Follow up service statement

## USER

*"Our greatest asset is the customer! Treat each customer as if they are the only one!"* Laurice Leitao

User was chosen for this chapter heading, but it's not just your prospect or customer, it encompasses a number of topics within your User (customer) such as: Customer Type, Customer values, DMU (Decision Making Unit). Often when we sell something, the person buying it will be the user hence the title, although this is not always the case and so we need to be mindful in our approach. But in short, it's important you have a 360 view of your customer because it will inform your strategic approach to them i.e. what type of product/service offering is likely to be accepted well, enhances your credibility with them, rather than pitching the wrong product feature/benefit/solution because you have not understood who you are selling to. An example of this would be selling the clinical benefits to a procurement manager who is more interested in Cost and Service.

**Customer Type**

Who are you selling to? Do you know before the call? It could be: Procurement, Clinical nurse, Engineer, Retail manager, General public, Administration. An administration based manager is likely to have their eyes glaze over if you start talking about programing and Linux system support and SQL database. But if you discuss the shortening of the admin processes to speed up work rates with automated backup of customer data, linked to CRM systems to reduce input, they're likely to engage with you. On the other hand, the computer systems manager will probably like to discuss the SQL database system and the programming that supports it. So it important we are matching our value/sales pitches correctly to our customer.

Some of the value/sales pitch differences may vary wildly between our customers, but some may be subtle, for instance I deal with clinical procurement so everything is on the table that I speak to nurses about, and also procurement so price is important. The pure procurement managers, price is the main topic. But equally, recognising this difference is important for the best outcome for you and you customer. It's your job to choose the right sales messaging to the customer. Either through experience or discussion with colleagues, we can decide what is likely to be the best approach to the customer and also, the most likely topics that will come up. But we still need to be flexible and not assume this is correct. Ideally, you'll develop a sales pitch that may be more suitable for the specific customer type so you'll discuss: Value, service contracts, reliability, company backup in this field, and also, of course, price for procurement customers. In my medical industry we also have discussions with Clinical staff so we talk around, clinical pathways, reduced bed stays, patient outcomes, reduced pain, quicker healing, easier application Value and, of course, price. With some customers who aren't buyers but true users with no budget, we may talk about who Liverpool beat at football on Saturday☺. You see, for some customers, they are the ones actually using the system, so a good relationship with them can help influence a sale if they are asked their opinion of the product. More on this in the DMU section shortly.

**Customer values.**

So what do I mean by this, well Spectrio wrote a good article, 'The Harvard Business Review Top 30 Customer Values' to explain this well.

In the article "The 30 Things That Customers Really Value," Eric Almquist and his colleagues classified customer values into four categories.

Functional -- the qualities of the brand, product, or service
Emotional -- the way the brand, product, or service makes the customer feel
Life-Changing -- the way the brand, product, or service alters the life of the customer
Social Impact -- the way the brand, product, or service alters the life of others

The table below shows some examples of the individual value propositions that can be added to products, services or brand values.

| SOCIAL IMPACT: | LIFE-CHANGING: | EMOTIONAL: | FUNCTIONAL: |
| --- | --- | --- | --- |
| Self-transcendence | Provides hope | Reduces anxiety | Saves time |
| | Self-actualization | Rewards me | Simplifies |
| | Motivation | Nostalgia | Makes money |
| | Heirloom | Design/Aesthetics | Reduces risk |
| | Affiliation/Belonging | Badge value | Organizes |
| | | Wellness | Integrates |
| | | Therapeutic value | Reduces effort |
| | | | Sensory appeal |

The Harvard researchers believe that individual sources of value in these categories can be added to products and services to make them more desirable for customers.

Examples of Customer Values at a Healthcare Practice.

A dentist's office, for instance, that caters to busy professionals may focus on the values to reduce effort, design/aesthetic, and wellness. The values the dentist office could address are:

- Provide online booking and calling services to remind patients about their upcoming appointments (reduces effort).
- Improve their waiting room and create a beautiful, high-end space that feels more like a spa than a dentist's office (design/aesthetic).
- Form partnerships with other healthcare and wellness facilities to offer discounts and promote overall well-being (wellness).

Examples of Customer Values at a Hotel. Values are also relevant to businesses in the hospitality industry. A small boutique hotel may choose to incorporate: therapeutic, affiliation/belonging, and sensory appeal. The hotel could address these values by:

- Provide additional services such as massage, therapeutic yoga, spas, and meditation (therapeutic).
- Create a community by setting up an online group or in-person, annual event that is focused on the other values their property supports (affiliation/belonging).
- Offer themed hotel rooms that make guests feel as though they are in another time and place (sensory appeal).

To bring this back to a salespersons viewpoint, these values proposition can be used based on the customers values, so if a customer values efficiencies then FUNCTIONAL values are likely to appeal. Values statements of saving time whilst keeping things organised in order to make more revenue are likely to draw in your customer to your product/service. Whereas the customer who is looking for change and a new direction is probably more receptive to LIFE CHANGING values, so motivations and hope for a new way are more likely to resonate with them.

It would be worth spending some time to match your customers values to the 4 values set out and then review the potential value propositions you can match for a specific customer.

**DMU. Decision Making Unit**

From my experience, it is not often I sell to one person who can authorise a purchase. It is usual that there is a group or committee that has been given the responsibility to oversee the procurement of the product/service. It is usual the panel comprises of different people with different agendas. But at this point, I would urge you to absolutely confirm who is in this group, as they are your DMU or Decision Making Unit.

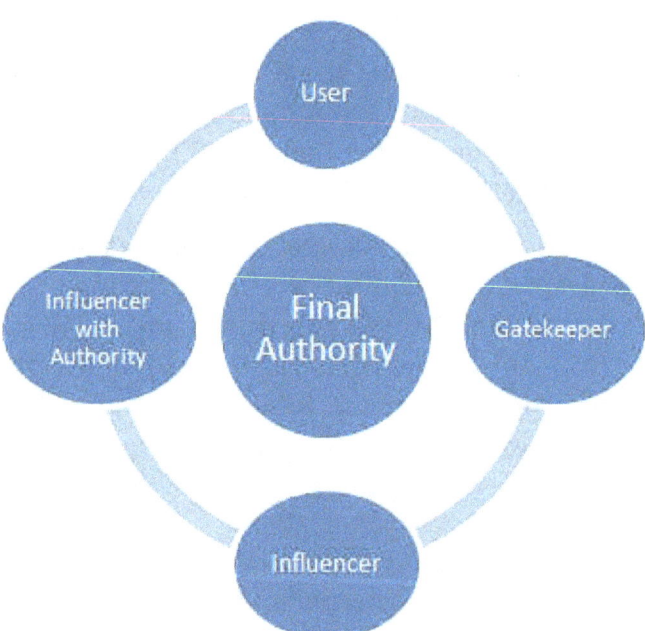

There are different versions of the DMU and I read online, it's a marketing biased tool, well I use it for my customers so let agree it's a sales tool☺. We'll use this one, as in the picture, as it's the type of customer set up I currently work with and so I know it has credibility. The DMU I use comprises of: Final Authority, Influencers with Authority, Influencers, Users and Gatekeepers. We'll have a look in more detail at each one:

**Gatekeepers**

The Gatekeeper could be responsible for the: data used to help create quotations, access to staff, making appointments and meetings within the decision making unit (DMU). The Gatekeeper needs to be on your side to allow for a smooth flow of the meetings and information you need in order to make create a good sales process.

*I found it useful to engage with gatekeepers using up-most respect and frankly some salespeople treat gatekeepers in a poor manner – hence they don't get access. If you think a sales manager doesn't talk to their receptionist at the office after an interview about the interviewee? They'll want to see how they acted with them, was there small talk, what was their manner like, then think again☺.*

## Users

Users are the people who are actually going to work with your product or services and they may well be involved in any trial of the product/service. Their opinion, therefore, is important and a relationship will need to be fostered. Often a questionnaire, for trial results for instance, are given out so these positive relations and responses are vital especially for handling difficult questions during a trial, so you need them 'on your side'. Ensure the Users have clarity and know how something works, so spend time with them to give the support they need. Time spent here is never wasted!

*I remember some people I discussed football with – Liverpool I think – they were the main porters in a hospital who were actually using the system I was trialing. I forged a good working relationship with them during the trial and headed off problems and provided solutions to make our sytsem work for them. You can also call them 'Users with Influence'. Because i I closely with them, we were able to iron out any trial issues so that by the end we actually showed a time saving in them doing their job. They actually liked using our system cause they had could take a break more easily because of the time saving!*

## Influencers

Influencers exert their experience and opinion on the trial/product or service. They are likely to be junior within the buying team and you need to have a rapport built with them. Meet with them and impart an understanding of what you (and the customer) are looking to achieve and how your proposal will benefit them and their workplace.

*Influencers though can come from any source – I had an influencer experience within Neuro-surgery where my current new prospect consultant had trained under one of my other key customers and so I discussed, without breaking confidences, some of the work I was doing with their old mentor. This further enhanced our relationship and my sales results. Now, officially not in the strict buying DMU department, an influencer just the same. Influencers will ordinarily be a person on the edge of the sales, whose input is still important and so not to be ignored.*

## Influencers with Authority

Influencers with Authority are often the senior people within the accounts buying process who have the experience to recognise a problem and try to find a solution. They will often be crucial in setting up meetings and initiating questions to you around your product/service. Firm value statements and solution statements will be needed to address their concerns well. As you can see, the FA will be likely to acting on the Influencers with Authority recommendations and so Influencers with Authority are likely to be your most important contacts in the decision making unit or DMU.

*Within National Health Service, wound care purchasing, new product selection is often carried out by trials, and the Influencers with Authority will be the ones setting up the trial parameters and the Users will carry out the actual trial. The trial data and results are fed back, often via Gatekeepers, to the Final Authority for sign off. This will only happen as long as FA and IwA are all in agreement hence why all people need to be involved with you.*

## Final Authority

The Final Authority is the actual person who has the power to authorise the sales or others will act on their recommendation to initiate an invoice. The Final Authority often negotiates about contract terms and will often be the driver for the parameters of the deal. They will no doubt consult with Influencers with Authority in order to set up trial rules or tender specs and will take their advice over whether to move forward with your product or service. The FA is a key person to gain a key relationship with and ensure your products/service value statements land well with them. It's worth saying again though, the FA may not be the key person in your sale, and they may be acting on advice from Influencers with Authority so you need to be aware of the fine lines within the DMU.

*The final Authority is likely to not act on their own and often will have support from 1 or 2 other key people and so it's important you keep an eye on who these people are. It's also interesting to know peoples backgrounds and other contacts in the industry they may know. Social media and networking is very valuable so try to get to know your customer.*

## DMU mapping

As an exercise, think of one of your key sales projects right now. It's useful to map out your key contacts there in the DMU. Who is the Final Authority, Who are the Influencers with Authority and Gatekeepers? Have you engaged with the Users?

So for each DMU type, score them as per the DMU relationship chart and be honest! If you're in the Low Relationship – High Influence stage then it's great that you know where you are, and can now action a better relationship strategy.

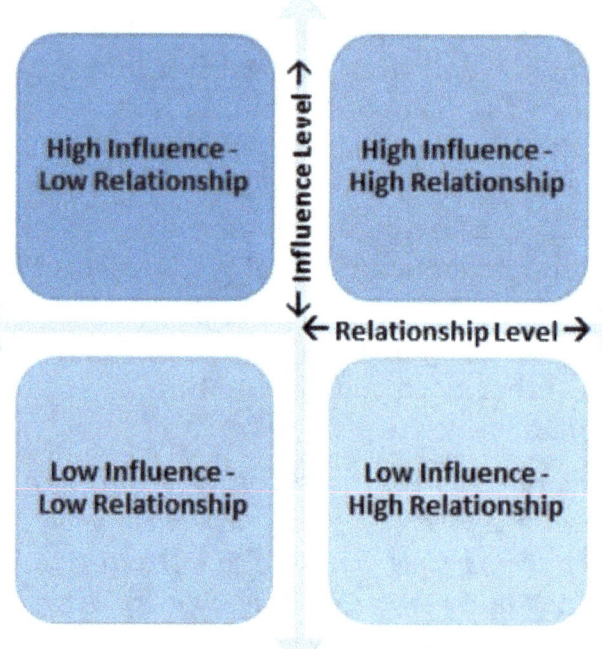

Of course, it makes sense that you need to be reaching for the High Influence – High Relationship for all your key DMU contacts and at least High Relationship for the others.

The fact that you can now see where you stand within a DMU, gives you the chance to make preperations and plans to push your relationships to the next level. You can also to adjust time spent with low influence contacts to increase time with the high influence contacts as this is where the real sales decisions will come from. This will give you better outcomes and sales results.

# YOUR UBER SALES CRAFT

## BEHAVIOUR

"Do not let the behavior of others destroy your inner peace." Dalai Lama

Recognising some of the behaviours of our customers can give us a heads-up on how to interact with them. If we do, we will get the most out of our time with our customer. It can take our relationship from a 0 to a 10 very quickly if we get it right! This means we are quicker to develop our relationship to a stage where they will act as advocates for us and even help sell our products for us. So what can we use to help us around this topic? One of the best methods I've come across, to understand a customer's behaviour, is to map their personality types and I use the following method regularly in my daily life.

**Personality Types**

For the system we'll use, there are 4 personality types:

- Talking

- Doing
- Controlling
- Supportive

And each type is given a colour

- Talking is Yellow
- Doing is Red
- Controlling is Blue
- Supportive is Green

Are you a Red, Blue, Green or Yellow personality type?

Here's a brief overview of each type.

**Reds:** tend to be strong leaders, fast paced thinkers, strong-willed, high energy, risk-takers, purposeful, drivers, competitive and rational. You may recognise many of the qualities in many leaders as they take ownership, need to be fast paced in their thinking, take risks and be purposeful and confident with it. They don't like waffle and tend to lack patience.

*If you have a Red customer they need just the facts and a clear, brief summary of what they'll get and won't want waffle, polite conversation and lots of data.*

**Blues**: are deep thinkers, analytical in nature, very detail focused and formal in their thinking. They can come across as being aloof, but they are deliberate in their approach and very systematic. They will be precise and pay attention to the detail you offer them and will be unlikely to make a decision without it. They will take their time in deliberating your proposal and are much slower paced than the reds or yellows. Blues like to have all the facts, and then logically put together an answer that is suitable. They don't like vagueness, a lack of detail or an absence of facts or figures.

*If you have a blue customer then ensure you have a logical sales process with all the supporting evidence and data you would need to back up you product and claims.*

**Greens**: tend to be more laid back, relaxed and patient. They are easy to get along with and very informal in their approach. Greens are social and focus on relationships so can come across as emotional. They are much slower paced in their thinking and are very democratic people. They're very understanding, and agreeable. They don't like 'pushy' and being put on the spot and can see if you're being insincere.

*So, if you have a green, focus on the well-being of others or how your product can help people but do this in a steady manner and go at their pace.*

**Yellows** are the chatty and outgoing ones who will talk with anyone. They are sociable, very imaginative, expressive and enthusiastic with it. Yellows are very informal, very optimistic and animated. Their Imaginations can sometimes run away with them as they are very fast paced thinkers. Yellows are very relationship focused and are visionaries with obvious high energy. They don't like their opinions being supressed or having too much detail. Your interactions with them must not be impersonal.

*If you spend time talking about holidays, cats, dogs etc then yellows will bond with you better as yellow don't want to be 'sold to'. Focus on how your product/service will help them is usually the best approach.*

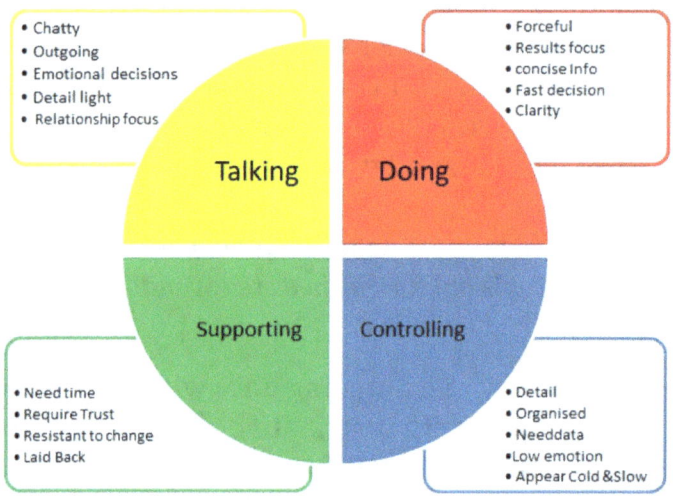

The above system is from a course I've been on a few time and it seems to be a variation of the Disc method of personality behaviour. It's been around since the 1920s and Disc uses four colours to explain types of personality: Red, Yellow, Blue and Green, which stand for Dominance, Influence, Conscientiousness and Steadiness, respectively. There are more complex tests for personality type but when you're in a stress situation, with a person in front of you, often the simpler the better. Most people are a mix of colours, but have one 'dominant' colour. Personally I'm a Blue with some Green.

I often write out for clarity who are the customers and what behaviour they match so I can bear this in mind when meeting with them in the future.

| Account Name: | St Julian Hospital | DMU Name | Type | Behaviour | Priority Need |
|---|---|---|---|---|---|
| Project Value: | £50,000 | Jane Smith | Final Authority | Red | Training |
| Product | Barrier cream | Dan Brown | Influencer with Authority | Blue | Training plan |
| Customer need/ Value proposition | Up skill staff and cost saving | Janice | Gatekeeper | Green | |
| Close date: | July XX | | | | |

Here are a few questions to help see what personality type you may be. Here's a 4 questions quiz for a quick test.

When you go to an event where there are many people you don't know, you're most likely to...

>  A) Make a beeline for the people most useful to me
>  B) Talk to as many people as possible
>  C) Stand off to the side and see if anyone comes to me
>  D) Find the few people I know and stick with them

When someone gives an opinion you disagree with, you're most likely to...

>  A) Tell them you disagree
>  B) Crack a joke and change the topic
>  C) Ask for more information
>  D) Nod and say nothing

There's a problem at work and people can't agree, you're most likely to say...

>  A) 'Let's make a decision'
>  B) 'Chill out, it'll be fine! '
>  C) 'Do we need more discussion?'
>  D) 'How does everyone feel?'

The best way you would describe yourself...

>  A) Motivated and decisive
>  B) Life of the party
>  C) Enjoy looking at data
>  D) Like helping others

**If you are mostly A's. You're a Red**

A Red tends to be a leader. You've got ambition and you're really good at getting the job done, but you can also be dominant – maybe a bit too pushy or impatient. You can clash with emotional Greens, who aren't as fast-paced as you, but give them encouragement and praise and they'll be a huge asset for you. You might feel impatient with Blues, who are always getting involved with loads of data but together you can do amazing work. You naturally get along well with a Yellow's energy; just remember they'll need to be happy to do their best work.

**If you are mostly B's. You're a Yellow**
Yellows are creative and are very social who can elevate everyone's mood, but you can also overwhelm a conversation with your anecdotes, and be a bit egotistical and undisciplined. The colour you're most likely to clash with is Blue, as they're all about the detail and will challenge you on it – so doing a bit more prep-work on a joint project will keep you both happy. Greens love your affectionate nature, but just remember to acknowledge their work and ask how they are. And with a Red, you will impress them with your big ideas, but keep the conversation short and sweet and they won't lose their patience.

**If you are mostly C's. You're a Blue**
Blues are often the calm ones in a team – you're level headed, hard-working and nothing is better for you than solving problems. But you can keep others at a distance, and be overly critical of people who haven't got a full brief of the problem. You can get irritated by Yellows, who seem to be all talk and no detail, but if you can accept your different qualities then together you can make an task or project 'take off'. Green colleagues for you are good; just remember that greens care as much about making people happy as you do about problem- solving. Yellows and Reds may both get impatient with your blue focus on getting things right, however, if you point out how this will help them be better at their jobs, everyone should be happy.

**If you are mostly D's. You're a Steady Green**

Greens are often the spine of any team– you are dependable, supportive and kind. But sometimes you can be too indecisive or compliant, which can frustrate others (especially if you're in a leadership role). You're most likely to have issues with Reds, who can seem aggressive or uncaring, but don't back away – do the opposite! They'll respond better if you are more direct. You naturally get on with Yellows; just don't get too involved in their drama. And if Blues seem a bit cold or standoffish, don't take it personally - just focus on the work and they'll respond best to your diligence.

## ENGAGE STRATEGY

*"Strategy is about setting yourself apart from the competition. It's not a matter of being better at what you do – it's a matter of being different at what you do."* Michael Porter

To this point we've looked at: You, Your Priorities, Your USP, Your value propositions, Your customer targets (Prioritise), Your customer types, Your customer values, Your Decision Making Unit and Your Customer behaviours, amongst other things. So for me, it always helps to get this written down and we don't have to write the whole thing out, but we should have clarity to demonstrate to our managers that we have our plan in order.

You should create your own record system to demonstrate you have your mind and customer strategy under control and have clarity of activities that needs to happen.

Map out and record the activities you need to prepare for to engage with the customer, and project at what point each will potentially take place. You can adjust these dates and details later once the customer has engaged with you, however top line engagement items can be planned for, such as:

> First meeting, what do we need to uncover, steer conversation
> Second meeting – re-address needs – confirm the solution
> Gain commitment to solutions
> Present proposal/Value propositions
> Agree trial, trial protocols
> Present trial data and outcome
> Close on needs and outcomes from trial
> Service agreement – education package agreements
> Monthly reporting to account.

Planning your strategic engagement is never time wasted and having a prepared plan in place that you can refer to, will keep you on track.

For your account objectives or goals that you want to achieve, make them SMART, Specific, Measureable, Achievable, Realistic and Timely.

Being able to refer to your strategic plan, for me, is important hence the 'plan on a page' approach. You should be able to write down on an A4 or Letter sized piece of paper the main strategy, value proposition, customer type, etc. with an overview of what you want to achieve from them.

We often have more than 10 customers we are actively engaging with so it's important to note and record where you are within the sales process and what the next steps are. Even though I recommend a paper version, you may be using a CRM such at Salesforce, com, Microsoft Dynamics, Sugar CRM and others so you need to be working with them to help you be organised. Often CRMs don't offer the versatility to note everything we have looked at hence making your own Strategy plan and maybe you can upload them to the account as your account strategy document. Should you leave the company there will be some useful information for the next person.

# RAPPORT

*"Rapport is the ultimate tool for producing results with other people. No matter what you want in your life, if you can develop rapport with the right people, you'll be able to fill their needs, and they will be able to fill yours."* Tony Robbins

What is Rapport?

A rapport is a connection or relationship with another person. It can also be defined as a state of harmonious relations with another individual or group. Building rapport can be defined as the process of developing a connection or relationship with another person. Good rapport is vital because it allows us to connect and build relationships with others, at personal and professional levels. It also helps establish a comfortable environment, both for work and life. Building rapport requires good use of social skills such as eye contact, sharing, cooperation, and listening. At the least, a good greeting, with a smile, to your customer such as, 'Hello, how are you, thank you for meeting with me today' with a firm handshake, will start you on the right road.

Here are a few pointers on how to develop rapport fast in your living and working environment.

**Research your customer.**

For you to have meaningful conversations, you need to know more about the person you are engaging with. Find out as much as you can about the individual e.g interests, likes, hobbies and background. Try also to get a 'warm' introduction from a work collegue or pier that you may have worked with.

**Good sources of information include:**

Their social media profile: Their LinkedIn page: A Google search, a corporate magazine is also worth obtaining if one is in reception.

Performing research on your customer helps uncover common ground and also makes room for shared experiences between the both of you and so enhancing your relationship.

**Actively listen**

Active listening involves giving your full attention to the individual you are meeting with. Active Listening is an important communication skill as it portrays the fact that you are giving them the attention they deserve. You want your customer to feel seen and heard — the more you show that you are actively listening to them, the more the other person is inclined to share.

When actively listening, make sure you are listening to understand, not just to give a response in a general way. Reflect on what is said and relate your question/statement or answer to what has been said.

**Ask questions**

One of the best ways to indicate that you are listening and are invested in the conversation is to ask questions. Asking follow-up questions during a conversation demonstrates interest that you genuinely want to understand the other person's point of view.

**Mirroring**

Mirroring and matching are techniques that aim at making you more like the other person. But go with caution here and don't be so obvious that you look like you are being false and even mocking them. Here are some examples of the techniques:

Watch your customer's body language e.g. posture and expression and try to match whatever they're doing. Use similar language to them. If they are using technical language, then a good idea would be to match this otherwise they may think you don't understand them. Match your customer's speech patterns including tone and tempo. If they are speaking at a low tempo, then soften your voice so that you are both using the same tempo.

### Be friendly

An important trait in rapport building is to be warm and approachable when meeting with your customer. The best way to go about this is to smile often. Smiling shows openness and also helps develop rapport with the other person. Another good tip is to make eye contact. It shows that you are listening and interested what the other party is saying. Be open to discussing information, find a balance in the amount of information you share about yourself. Be careful giving out personal information or relationship details, this would be unusual in a formal business setting. Use open handed gestures not fists nor pointing and keep your torso visible, not covered up. People in general, like to hear their name said within conversations, so use it periodically in your discussions, it will help gain that rapport we need.

### Personality Type

Now we are in front of our customer, we'll start to be able to uncover and see the Behaviour Personality types we looked at earlier. In brief – are they a Red, Blue, Green, Yellow?

So a quick review of them.

**Reds:** tend to be strong leaders, fast paced thinkers, strong-willed, purposeful, drivers, competitive and rational.

**Blues**: are deep thinkers, analytical in nature, very detail focused and formal in their thinking.

**Greens**: tend to be more laid back, relaxed and patient.

**Yellows**: are chatty and outgoing ones who will talk with anyone.

**The VAK Model**

There are a great many different ways of categorising learning styles, but Neil Fleming's VARK model, introduced in 1987, is one of the most popular.

According to the VARK model, learners are identified by whether they have a preference for:

Visual learning (pictures, movies, diagrams)

Auditory learning (music, discussion, lectures)

Reading and writing (making lists, reading textbooks, taking notes)

Kinesthetic learning (movement, experiments, hands-on activities)

Because we are using this in terms of a meeting then the Reading and writing is not so applicable so we'll look more towards, Visual, Auditory and Kinesthetic for our sales calls.

**Visual customers** are more likely to learn and be receptive by seeing things. So we need to adapt how we present ourselves to them. In our presentation and discussion we should focus on word associated with sight, and so "I see", "you see how this", "picture a way that" are the types of phrasing that will work well with visual customers.

**Auditory customers** are more likely to learn and be receptive by hearing/listening to things. So, as before, we need to adapt how we present ourselves to them. In our presentation and discussion we should focus on word associated with auditory and the also tone of voice we use, and so "I hear you", "If I can tell you a way", "if this sounds good" are the types of phrasing that will work well with auditory customers.

**Kinesthetic customers** are more likely to learn and be receptive by feeling/touch things. They may remember things by walking through them. In our presentation and discussion we should focus on words associated with walking through something, and so "If I could tell you of a solid way to save budget...", "if this feels good for you, can we...", are the types of phrasing that will work well with kinesthetic customers.

## YODA

Not this Yoda!

YODA was described in *'Body Language - It's What You Don't Say That Matters'* by Robert Phipps.

YODA is a great way to remember that, what you see within the customer meeting; you have an opportunity to change things if you want.

**Y**ou – You have to be fully engaged with your customer.
**O**bserve – Notice things you didn't before.
**D**ecode – Work out what it all means.
**A**dapt – Change your behaviour and wording to get better results.

**You:**

Now I have to say at this point that some people are absolutely awful at reading the signs people send, and there are those that are good at reading it. Generally the good ones seem to know just how to react or behave in any situation. More often than not, they look comfortable with themselves. People warm to them because they feel at ease in their company. They exude confidence. Whether you are good at reading body language right now or not, you will understand that *you* are the key to how people react around you. You also have choices about how you react to *them*, but only if you learn to Observe more...

**Observe:**

Observation is the starting point for reading body language. Once you can read it, you have options with what to do with the information.

So let's use 'lying' as an example.

If you know someone is lying to you because you've been observing the changes in their body language, you have the choice of calling them out on it, or just tucking that bit of information away for future reference. If you're oblivious to it then you have no choice, you have to go along with the lie. This can cost you in all sorts of ways: financially, emotionally, and even spiritually. Let's face it; no one likes being taken for a mug.

In business, the truth is not always told and it's sometimes deliberately withheld. For example, in negotiations you don't give away everything up front. You withhold certain information for later, releasing it at an opportune moment.

The more observant you are, the more adept you will be at avoiding pitfalls, spotting untruths and understanding when you've pushed a situation to the limit. Often you just need to listen to your 'gut instinct' as often it is correct, but you must allow yourself this option and not be too stressed and preoccupied to notice it.

**Decode:**

A close link to observing is decoding. It's essential that you develop the skills to decode what you are seeing. That way, you stay in control and have the opportunity to choose how to handle a situation.

Decoding starts at the beginning, when you meet someone. Whether it's the first meeting or the fifty first, a person's body language, like their moods and attitudes, changes from moment to moment depending on what's being talked about. They'll have an opinion on what you are saying. If they like it, their body language will be open, positive and encouraging. But if you suddenly stray onto a tricky subject where you have opposing views, the body language will change in an instant.

Truth teller's heart and blood pressure stay in a nice comfortable relaxed zone when the topics are non-controversial, but introduce any controversy, the heart rate and blood pressure rise almost instantly.

What's interesting is that when a customer is relaxed and comfortable, body language is fluid, it usually mirrors the other person. But, as discussed, as soon as any controversy sneaks in, the body language changes. When asked to try to maintain the mirroring, people find it extremely difficult and their body movements become more jerky and angular. You might have noticed this in yourself or others. It's the changes in body language that are the keys to look out for. It was the subject matter being discussed that probably caused this change – what was that? What could be there issue?

A quick example is the hand and wrist. When relaxed and fluid, the hand rolls loosely at the pivot point of the wrist. This stops the moment someone starts gets more serious about something. At this point, their hand, wrist and forearm begin to move as one, pushing forward with jabbing, sweeping gestures.

If you observe this, you are in a position to decode it and make sense of it. In this situation, a sudden rigidity in someone's gestures would tell you that whatever was just said or done, prior to the change, is important to that person. With this insight into their thoughts, you then have the option either to go back and cover it in a different way or change the subject completely and talk about something less important or controversial.

**Adapt:**
You will have picked up by now that the greatest gift to come from understanding someone through their body language is that it gives you choices. It gives insight into how they are feeling at any moment. Once you've learned to tap into someone's emotions, you can build a much deeper level of trust and rapport with them. In business, that means people are more likely to enjoy working with you.

Adapting can only be done if you observe and decode first.
Adapting can bring surprising results very quickly.
Adapting is your free choice.

But what exactly is adapting? Adapting means changing your default reaction to something more consciously designed to shift the other person from their position to a different one – one that will be better for you.

We do this all the time, in most cases without realising that we've already been through the process of observing and decoding a set of signals to get there. Here's a really simple example. Let's say two guys are standing face to face talking about football and one is winding the other up about the results the previous Saturday. The butt of the jokes starts to get annoyed and their body language changes; eyes glare, teeth become gritted, shoulders are tensed and fists clench. It's a physical reaction which says, "Don't push me or I'm going to explode."

If you've noticed it, which you almost certainly would because that particular set of signals spells danger, you have a choice right there and then, whether to keep pushing their buttons or back off. Unless you want them to vent their anger, you'd be a fool to keep pushing. Sometimes in a fight it's better just to back down.

That's the adapting part. This is an extreme example, but as you can see, it's not rocket science. It's often what we do automatically.

**Focus Points**

The main Focus points for gaining Rapport are;

   Look at their body language

   Actively listen

   Find common ground

   Address their personality type

   YODA

You should also reflect on the first call before attending a second call in order to ensure you have the correct approach to the customer in a way they will be receptive. We need to act on what we learn from our customers. This has been referred to as the Call Continuum in the CoachHouse APPROACH™ sales training. This is a good way to focus your mind on building Rapport with your customer quickly.

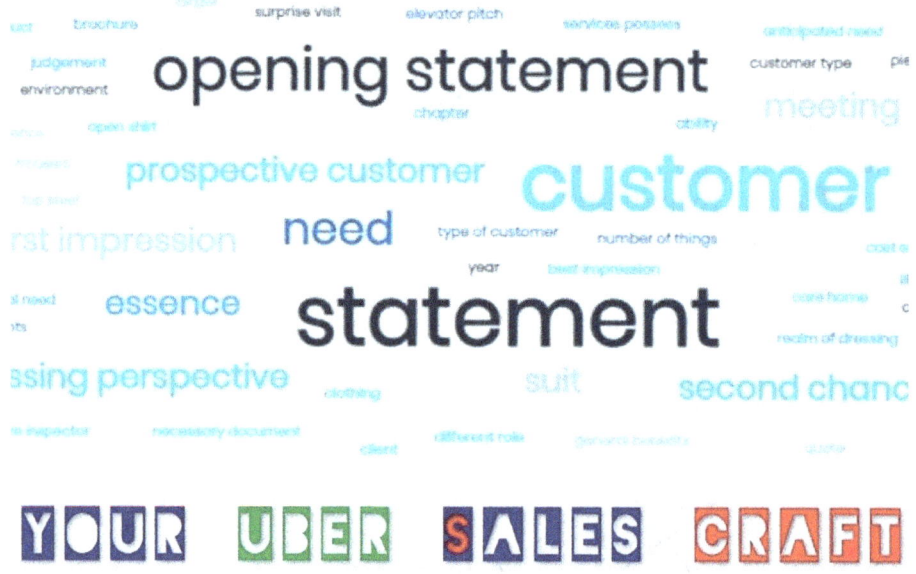

## STATEMENT

*"You never get a second chance to make a first impression." Will Rogers*

Statement means a number of things within this chapter, making a statement from a dressing perspective, but also your opening statement to your prospective customer.

**From a Dressing perspective**

Let's look at Statement as in 'making a statement'. So we're in the realms of dressing appropriately for the customer and the environment you are in. 'You never get a second chance to make a first impression' so let's do what we can to make the best impression we can.

So let's not assume it would be best if we all wear a 3 piece suit or best skirt and blouse. For some customers this may well be what's expected, but some customers we can be less formal and ensure we aren't putting our customer into an 'anxious' state.

*For years I wore a suit and tie to work but when I changed to a different role and called on care homes, it became very apparent that I was over-dressed, even hearing comments that they thought I was a healthcare inspector (CQC) on a surprise visit! And yes they were concerned upon first seeing me. So now I wear tidy trousers, open shirt and blazer, far more relaxed and open for this customer type!*

In essence, use your judgement to dress appropriately for the type of customer you are meeting with.

But it doesn't end with your clothing – being prepared with brochures, quotes and other necessary documents show that you are professional, prepared and that the customer will have confidence in your ability to work professionally with them. You should be making a statement about yourself and your conduct.

**Opening statement to your prospective customer.**

*A strong confident opening statement will always set up the meeting well, rather than an ill thought out weak one.*

It's useful; if your prospect has not heard of you, to have an opening statement that can be tailored to entice your prospect to want to know more about you. This can also be related to your elevator pitch but it's important that you pitch this statement to the anticipated needs of your customer. Don't be too specific, but keep it to the general benefits your company/service possesses such as: improved… efficiencies in… cost savings… We are yet to uncover the client's actual needs so need to keep this 'top level'.

In essence, your opening statement would contain:
Who you are
The company you're from
What you offer (top level)
Benefits to your prospect (generalised)
A question to engage your prospect

For instance, an opening statement like, 'I'm Brian Gwyther from

Acme Holdings and we have been successful for 15 years in this industry supporting business like yours by increasing efficiencies whilst reducing operating costs. I am pleased you were able to meet with me today as I would like to understand more about your business and to find out how we can work together. Can you tell me about……'. Give clarity of who you are and why you are there in front of them. It's important to spend some time on reviewing what these types of opening statements look and sound like for your business and rehearse them so they become second nature.

But also remember to try and make it as natural as possible and not too scripted which is why you'll need to adjust this statement to match the personality of the prospective customer and your own. This is why the small talk is important before your opening statement, that's when you 'get down to business'. For a more relaxed and upbeat customer your opening statement may be more, 'You know, we've been doing this for 15 years and have helped customers in the next town achieve savings and efficiencies in spite of issues around the new legislation within the industry.' This truly is a statement, not a question, but what it achieves is a more conversational start and prompts a response from the customer. So, when in the next section, ASK, we discuss questioning, and we do want to avoid an interrogation. Statements showing agreement or unity are useful to keep the customer relaxed and still talking.

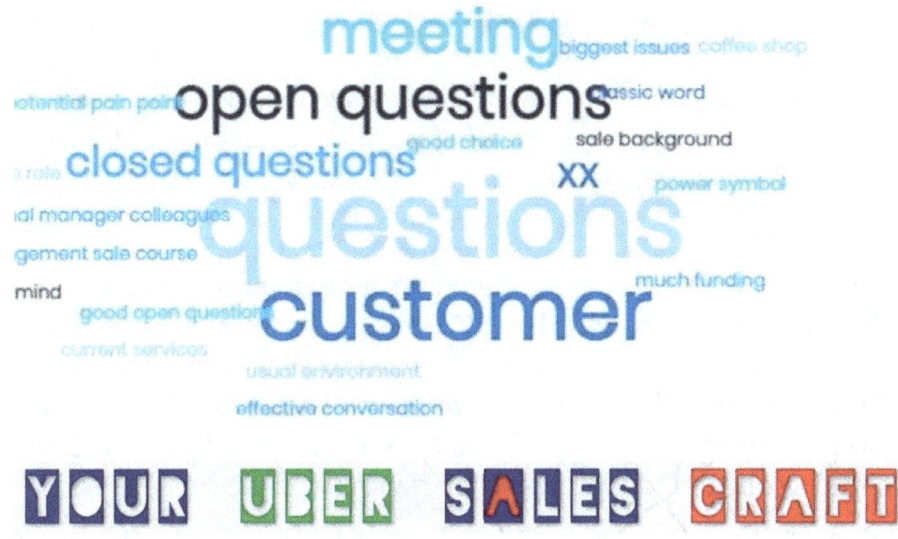

# ASK

*"The art and science of asking questions is the source of all knowledge."*
Thomas Berger

When we are with our customer, we need them to be open and honest about their business or needs, so it's important they are as relaxed and as communicative as they can be. We need to not just jump straight into questions with no let up. We need to have formed our rapport with them to get to the stage where we can have an effective conversation.

As an aside, where we ASK our questions can be important to. We usually have these meetings in their office, but this is where they have the 'power', why not try to get them to 'neutral' ground, away from distractions and all their power symbols like awards and their big chair☺. A restaurant, coffee shop or somewhere similar would be a good choice. This way they will relax more and be able to focus more on you outside of their usual environment.

## The basics of open and closed questions

*It was a surprise to me, as someone from a sales background, that when on a management sales course, my Operational manager colleague, hadn't heard of open and closed questions. We take them for granted but they are very important within our sales role but are not necessarily widely known about.*

## Open questions

The classic words most associated with open questions are: who, what, where, when, why, how. They are also known as the 5W's and 1H and they are designed to be used to elicit information and build a picture of what your customer's issues are. The expectation is that you will gain information from using these questions to find a solution for your customer with your product or service.

Some good open questions I have come across are: What is your motivator in meeting with me today? Why are you looking to change your current service? What improvements would you like within XX?

What aspect of my introduction/mailer/brochure interested you most? What are you hoping to achieve by the end of our meeting? Where do think you can gain improvements in…? Where is the biggest issue within your business right now? How much of an issue is XX to you? How much funding is available for this Project? (Hey, you never know, they might tell you!!)

In order to get your customer to talk, you will have to ask questions that you already know, or think you know, the answer to. It's always good to have a customer confirm your thoughts. You can also use your questions to steer the conversation toward potential pain points that you have a solution to and bring this to the front of your customers mind.

Why – I've always been cautious about how this question is used as we must not infer that the customer has made a buying mistake in the past as egos may be bruised. If you use a question such as 'Why did you decide to use/buy x product or service?' be careful on your response to this as they may have made the decision and now it's not working out for them. For some customers, it's better to not comment, than or pass judgement or agree they made a mistake!

## Closed Questions

Closed questions are usually used to confirm a point or marker within a conversation. They can also be used to stress a point of importance e.g. 'Is it correct that if you don't have XX in place on the 1st of next month you will incur a penalty?'

Close questions should, officially, only be answered with a 'Yes' or 'No' and their use should be to get a point of closer or agreement. For instance, a useful point to ask a customer using a closed question could be, 'if we can come to an agreement today, is there anyone else I need to see to discuss the proposal? Whilst this isn't strictly a Yes/No answer, it does prompt a brief answer that is likely to start with a Yes or a No. This question is also a check to see if the person in front of you has the authority to make a deal with you.

This isn't always the case; it never fails to amaze me of celebrity interviewers asking closed questions and the guest talking a lot for an answer. This is fine if your customer is a 'yellow' but don't expect a 'Red' to treat a closed question with more discussion. We need to use them appropriately and frankly, professionally.

## Not an Interrogation! TEDEE

There are some other questioning words that can soften the potentially endless: Who, What, Where, When questions. These are words used to elicit a description within the answer such as: Tell me about, Explain to me, Describe the situation, Expand for me, Elaborate on... It would be useful, once a pain point is exposed by the usual closed and open questions, to ask the customer to elaborate on it. This can help us to understand the point more fully. But this isn't their only use, you can use them to get the customer talking in place of a Who, What, Where, When question. So if we take some of our open question examples, we can transform them to the TEDEE types:

What is your motivator in meeting with me today? Becomes 'Tell me about your motivation in meeting me today?'

Why are you looking to change your current service? becomes 'Describe for me what you're looking to change in your current service?'

What improvements would you like within XX? becomes 'Explain for me the improvements you would like within XX?'

We can see that the slight difference in the question makes them more conversational and less like an interrogation.

**Statements**

Statements can also be a useful tool when making a point or trying to entice some more information. It is usual that a person will either agree or disagree with a statement and so without asking a question, they will still offer information but without you asking a question. For instance, 'Covid 19 has hit businesses hard and so many staff have been laid off now'. 'I've helped the Acme Company recently with their engineering service to make their booking system more efficient'. 'The legislation change has hampered a lot of businesses'. It would also be beneficial to use open body language with nods, good eye contact or upward inflection of speech at the end of the statement to indicate openness within the statement.

These are great ways to keep the conversation going and information still flowing and for many people they will work fine. Now for a person who is not naturally chatty these may now work well as they won't naturally recognise it as a conversation, so use them wisely.

Just a point of note here, so often have I been with sales people who use the 'scatter gun' effect of talking – throwing in all the feature and benefits of their product and hoping something sticks. Usually it doesn't as you are not 'selling'. Ask the questions and sell to the solution you have uncovered for their problem or need.

# LISTEN

*"I like to listen. I have learned a great deal from listening carefully. Most people never listen." Ernest Hemingway*

Some say that Listening is the greatest skill a sales person possesses. Unlike those who can 'sell sand to Egypt', they tend to be talkers and have not asked or listened to their customers issues and so have no idea what the customer wants or needs – no solution is therefore offered.

Listening is important as people want to be heard. If you give your prospective customer this courtesy, they will remember you and will want to work with you. This could be the difference between you and your competitor, the fact that you have formed a better relationship by understanding their needs in a far more intricate way.

In order to achieve this relationship, it is vital to take note of the answers from your open questions, closed questions and statements. Reflect on them and note them, demonstrating active listening, as discussed in the Rapport section of this book. Sometimes you will need to reaffirm back to your customer what you are hearing to show you have understood them. This will show your customer you are taking in what they are saying with a logical process. This reassures them you are in tune with their situation. Incidentally I always have a notebook with me to write down what the main points are of a meeting. I then also use this to read back to the customer their points to demonstrate this understanding. For forgetful people like me ☺ this is a great tool.

*However, the use of a notebook was taught to me during a negotiation course and it's visual message of, being open or closed, actively writing, stop writing, can be a useful tool to send a message to the customer (or employee) on your thoughts and can help reinforce a point.*

Keep a note of issues in a methodical and organised manor so avoiding confusion. If there are multiple pain points for the customer, try to get them to priorities them, which would they want fixed first? As this forms the main solution for them and you'll need to formulate the responses related to these.

Whilst in the 'listening mode' you should not be interrupting the customers speech flow as you could be cutting off some useful information. You should also be thinking on what they are saying in order to make a suitable response to delve deeper or affirm what they are saying to show understanding. Keep good eye contact and don't allow distractions – phone on silent etc.

Also, Listen to their emotions – if you have your appointment and it becomes obvious your customer is unable to relax because they are mid-crisis or something has happen that is taking their attention it could be better for you in the long run, to offer to meet them again when you can have their attention in a better and more positive way. Never be afraid to postpone a meeting if the prospective customer is not in a 'good place' to take the meeting. That said this situation is rare and not usual but you will gain some brownie points for recognising this. Live to fight another day.

*I was meeting with Theatre Manager and they had just lost a patient on the operating table and, understandably, it was obvious that the staff around us and my customer were in some distress. I offered to reschedule the meeting and they were grateful that I did so. Not that you want to gather 'brownie points' but the customer now 'owed me one'. Our next meeting went very well as they were already grateful to me and thank me again.*

# EXPLAIN

*"Everything is complicated if no one explains it to you."* Fredrik Backman

Explain is simply explaining how your product or service matches the customer's needs, this is also known as Needs Matching.

So in the A.L.E section, we have uncovered their needs by ASKing and understood them by LISTENing so now we need to formulate the best responses possible to EXPLAIN how we can match those needs.

We need to be very specific in taking the customer needs in turn, by priority to the customer, to show how our product or service is able to meet those needs. For a product and service related sell we could use the tried and trusted F.A.B.

**Features:** – are facts/features about the product/service
**Advantages:** – what are the advantages to the customer of your

product or service?

**Benefits** – what personal/business benefits does the customer receive from it?

Feature - Advantage – Benefit.

You need to know the FAB of your product so that for each feature, you know the advantage and so the benefit for your customer.

There's also an old saying around this – 'Features tell, Benefits sell.' It is important to not just list a load of features to your customer such: it's red, it's got this button, has this setting, as they don't relate to your customer's needs. Ensure you are discussing the benefits to the customer using/utilising what you're selling.

Make sure you know the benefits of what you are selling.

So for a simple example let's take a Washing Machine and create our FAB

**Features:** You're selling washing machines, the features of a washing machine are 120 high by 85 cm wide, colour: white, can wash an 8kg load. Spin speed is 1800 RPM

**Advantages:** It is a standard sized washing machine, and the colour matches other 'white goods'. The clothing is very dry when it spins with 1800 RPM and can carry a family wash amount

**Benefit:** Installing a washing machine gives more free time for you, time you can spend together or a cafe owner saves the time an employee has to wash the table cloths by hand, time that now can be used to clean the kitchen. You can save time because of the larger load of clothes the machine can take, you need less washing sessions.

So an example statement could be,' You mentioned that you have a large family and often time is tight so this machine holds an 8kg clothing load which means you only need run the washing cycle once rather than spending time doing 2 loads. This will free you up to spend more time with your family and reduce the washing day burden'.

Within my current industry of healthcare, we'll be discussing 'the patient's skin protection afforded by the silicone barrier cream that last for 3 washes to ensure the patient has a lasting protection from moisture damage on their skin.' It doesn't matter what the product or service is, FAB works very well.

So the Feature is: Silicone in the barrier cream, Advantage is: it protects the skin for 3 washes, the Benefits is: that it offers long skin protection from moisture damage.

**Which FAB?**

A feature may have a number of advantage/benefits. If there are multiple A-B's then you need to choose the right one to land best with your customer. Now, depending on the customers response in the ASK section, will inform you on which FAB to present.

So if the customer need is price – we focus on values to justify price, if it's a specific feature we don't spend time talking about other features, we sell to the one they want/need.

Some of the more experienced people out there will be saying now, 'sell them what the need, not what they want' and this is true, the customer though has to come with you on the 'sales journey', they need to see that what they need is actually, now, what they want.

**Pre-close**

Now we're getting good! If, through all your questioning, you know you have the customers' needs met then you could pre-close them with a question such as, 'if I can demonstrate to you that we can satisfy all your needs/requirement, would you be prepared to sign with me today?' This is also known as the Hypothetical Close.

*When I was a young sales person I was taking part in role-play and, of course, being fed all the needs I had a Feature Advantage Benefit for, and I missed this golden opportunity to pre-close them before stating promptly that we could meet the needs. There was an air of disappointment on the manager's face that I didn't preclose (but I didn't know what that was at the time!), even though he was laughing, but none the less, don't be in too much of a rush to close your customer. This stayed with me for over 30 years.*

## SUMMARIES

*"Perhaps the best test of a man's intelligence is his capacity for making a summary."* Lytton Strachey

Summaries are a great way to describe, to your customer; you have their needs in order, covered, met and answered. You are giving them confidence that you have understood what they want and need and are in a position to help match this and move the customer to a better place within themselves and their business, buying from you.

So a summary such as, 'we have discussed the financial aspect of our offering and you agreed the saving was what you needed within the project, coupled with the increased output you gain through the advanced technology you'll be investing in……..' the next statement or question should be the Close.

We can also use the summary to move a customer to a specific aspect of the call to help clarify and make crystal clear the main benefit. A summary like 'Following our discussions, I think you would gain the most benefit from …….. that our product brings' or 'Could I re-iterate that "the feature" our service offers you, would gain you the most value.'

However, we may not have been able to move so seamlessly to get to this stage. The customer may well have raised some 'Objections' or points of clarification. They will need to be addressed and as a rule, I tend to deal with objections when they arise. I have been on courses where they say to get the customer to 'park' it till a later point but personally, if I was the customer, it would nag at me that my concern wasn't addressed. So I address it so we can move forward with a customer who now has a 'happy mind'. There may well be certain times such as if you are presenting on PowerPoint that you want to discuss issues raised at the end, then this is fine as this is a different scenario and handling objections from a group can often spin out of control if you aren't careful. You must maintain order in these situations.

**Objections**

I have to say, I love Objections! And it's for a number of reasons:

The customer has been interested enough to think of an issue.

The customer wouldn't interact if they weren't interested.

I'm now in a true partnership with the customer to resolve their issue.

The customer issues, once answered, only leaves one action – to buy!

The objection could be on price, a missing feature, service requirements, supply route issue. Whatever the issue, we tend to deal with them using the **LARA** method.

> **Listen**: Listen and understand what the objection is. In many cases objections are 'False objections' and these are where there has been a miscommunication or failed listening, and confusion has crept in – these are easily put right. Other may

be 'Factual Objections' and these need to be address often with building up the other positive benefits of your system to make up for any short fall.

**Accept**: Ensure both you and your customer are in agreement of what the objection is. So, repeat the objection back and confirm that both of you are clear on what it is.

**Resolve**: This is a great opportunity for you to discuss the issue more fully and you can bring to the fore more company information that may help resolve the situation or find a way that you company could help resolve it.

**Agree**: After identifying and solving the issue you need to agree to move forward now this issue is resolved.

## Price

Price is often an objection and critically so, if you are more expensive. If you are, then you must justify this with discussion of value, service, add-on, Apps, service engineers, specialist support and all the value related extras. Where possible, before your customer objects to price, you need to have built up the total picture of your service or benefits and their needs. If you are asked early on in the call for the price you'll need to get a delay and ask that your service and product be discussed so that the customer can more fully realise the pricing of your product or service. However, if you cannot avoid discussing the price early on in the call, then justify it with your value statements and benefits of your product for the customer. A nice statement to use if you have to state the price early, is 'The price is £xxx and I will now demonstrate to you why this is good value for you and your company.'

Price on one hand is a major objection but also think of it this way, the customer has to realise the value they gain but using your product is worth the price, so our job is to ensure that the customer perception is crystal clear on the value you can offer them. Any doubt and they won't be buying. Value is very subjective to people but value can be expressed by this formula:
*VALUE = Benefit to the customer MINUS Cost of purchase*

Ensure you are creating the right value points to the needs of your customer and you will have more successes than losses.

A cautionary note – not every sales call ends with a sale. It is important that if you cannot overcome some objections, you take lessons from it and leave on good terms with the customer as one day your service or product will evolve to satisfy the issue – or at least the customer retires or moves on and someone more reasonably joins☺. Believe me, this is a thing!

# CLOSE

*"You Don't Need A Big Close As Many Sales Reps Believe. You Risk Losing Your Customer When You Save All The Good Stuff For The End. Keep The Customer Actively Involved Throughout Your Presentation, And Watch Your Results Improve."* Harvey Mackay

Closing is the easiest part of the process if you have covered off well, all that goes before it. The close is the point where we need to gain a final commitment from our customer. We will have been looking for nods, approving statements from our customer, answering queries and questions and now we need to close off this conversation with a positive conclusion.

**Types of closing**

There are a number of types of closing that exist and in time you will find you favour a particular way of closing that suits your style and product/service. Here's a few of the more common closing types:

Trial Close
Direct Close
Assumptive Close
Alternative Close
Hypothetical Close
Higher Authority Close
Fear Close

**Trial Close (Preclose)**

This isn't a true close but will prompt a buying signal to test the water with where the customer is at in their buying process. 'What do you think about what we have discussed so far?', 'Does this look like the solution you need?'

**Direct Close**

The direct close is as it say – really quite direct and to the point. If the customer is of the type who will take directness then, 'Can I ask you sign the order today?', or 'Are you happy to go ahead placing the order?' will be fine with them.

**Assumptive Close**

The assumptive close is best used where there has been agreement all the way and no real objections have been found. You also have no reason think that, to this point, they wouldn't buy it. So if you have a happy and content customer, 'I'll call the office to check the stock levels ready for your order?' or 'Will you pay by card or cheque?' would seem appropriate.

**Alternative Close**

I quite like this one ☺. The classic is, 'Do you want Red or Blue?!' It's giving a customer you think is positive a buying format option. Its part assumptive but is also offering alternatives. They could be, 'Would you like 1 shipment drop or split over 3?' or 'Would you like to pay in full for an additional 3% discount or pay off in instalments?'

## Hypothetical Close

We touched on this earlier and the hypothetical close is where you ask the question to the customer that gives some options for the customer to choose from. If you like your programing or Excel formulas, it's an 'If..Then' statement.

'If we included a 2 year warranty and 5 year servicing, then could you recommend our service to your committee?

This is also a good way to handle an objection; if you answer their objection, then let's look to gain approval to move forward to purchase.
'If I can fully answer the quality issue that you have raised, would you be prepared to sign with me today?'
I think it's a great way to understand the mind-set of your customer and if you're likely to gain the sales.

## Higher Authority Close

This close allows you to refer to a higher authority for approval of your deal to the customer.

'I have given you my best offer possible, if I can get the free 1st service approved by my manager, do we have a deal?'

Now, I'm not saying this is an 'unethical tactic' if used knowing you can offer the deal, you may well need to talk to your boss. If you need added authorisation for a deal then fine, but be honest in how you treat customers.

## Fear Close

Good one this! If there a shortage of stock, an issue present or there is a time pressure for the customer, this is a situation that could work in our favour. This could be one of the situations where it is easier for you to have the 'power' within a sales process as not only does the customer have a problem to solve, they are running out of time to. If you can help, then you don't need to discount etc. to sweeten the deal, you can just solve it for them at a great profit margin. I would expect you to be building the consequences of their situation and issues for them for not buying with you.

*I was with a customer during a tender deal and the procurement team was proposing to my Senior nurse customer they only awarded me one of our products in the offering, the other type to a competitor. So I sat with the clinical customer and discussed with her the issues. She and I would face issues over split training programs - that would she would have to organise, 2 companies training within one treatment area, as well as the confusion over the educational posters and clinical pathways that now needed to be developed by 2 companies. Thankfully I had a great relationship with her; she picked up the phone to the procurement lead and started the process to get us placed as first line for both products.*

There's a saying within the sales community of: ABC – Always Be Closing. Talking about Feature and Benefits is important but you need to be gaining commitment from your customers to earn your commission so don't be afraid to close, and you know, the customers will expect you to.

Always try to close on a Win-Win for you and your customer; you want repeat business and lasting relationships with your customers. If you get 'Hardwired' into their business as a supplier then it's harder for them to let you go and switch to another supplier.

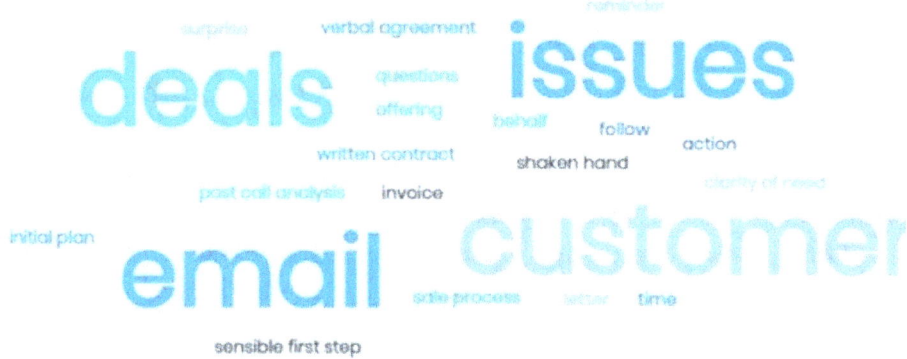

## REINFORCE

*"The way positive reinforcement is carried out is more important than the amount."* B. F. Skinner

One you have agreed on a deal and shaken hands, you need to reinforce what you have agreed and get it written down and emailed at least, so that there can be no follow-up issues. An email or letter stating the verbal agreements and offerings made will be a sensible first step, ahead of any formally written contracts or invoices especially if they take time to be organised. These emails can also serve as a reminder to your customer of any actions they agreed to take on behalf of the deal.

You should also conduct a post call analysis on the sales process you just had: did you open well? Was there clarity of need? Were your questions good enough to get to the issues quickly? Was the close professional? But you can also ask; Was your initial plan and approach to the customer correct? Were there any surprises and how would you better overcome them again?

## AGREEMENT

*"All I wanted – was agreement with all my desires after a constructive discussion." Winston Churchill*

Once everything is formally agreed, it's now time for you to follow any service contract or training that you have agreed upon. It's critical that if there is a service element to your sale that either you or say, a service manager, looks after the agreements made with your customer. If you have a service manager you may well need to have regular contact with them in order to monitor how the servicing is going to regularly meet with the customer to report on this.

**No-cost Value Added Service**

*In a previous company we added a no cost service line to invoices, if the company had agreed certain services for free, we could always show what the value was of the service on the invoice even though we no-costed it. Additional services have value and you are within your rights to show what the customer gets, even though there's no charge for it.*

# FOLLOW UP

*"Diligent follow-up and follow-through will set you apart from the crowd and communicate excellence." John C. Maxwell*

Making a follow-up call or visit after a sale is completed is important for a number of reasons, including improving yours and your business's credibility. It will add value to the service or product the customer purchased from you and gives you an opportunity to build a relationship that could lead to additional sales from the same customer and also referrals to more potential clients.

When engaged in the initial selling process, we let our customer know the purchase was in their best interests. If that was true, then our enthusiasm shouldn't diminish. Instead, we should continue to support their decision and strengthen the fact that they made the right decision.

**Post-sale problems**

Returns are a pain for salespeople, and the closer our relationship is with our customer, the less likely it will be a major issue as we would hope to be able to manage it well with our good customer. We should always make sure that post sales training is completed so that all staff have been trained and less likely to cause us any user error issues.

Ensure deliveries go smoothly and all products are working well. Use technical support if available and reassure clients that support is available if they have any further questions. Become a resource for your customers, who will not only call when they have a problem, but think of your business when they need additional products or services.

**Kindness and respect**

We should follow-up after the sale to thank customers for their business. We can never have enough happy customers. We need to make a positive impression on customers for them to use you again and recommend you to their network of contacts.

**Sell - Sell - Sell!**

The ultimate goal of following up after a sale, is to generate more sales. Customers are far more likely to purchase from someone they trust and provides excellent customer service. Once you've build a great relationship, you should ask for referrals. We need to use the follow-up call to explain any incentives your business may offer for referrals and assure customers that everyone you serve receives the same consideration and follow-up care.

Set a schedule for yourself to contact former clients on a regular basis to keep your business name in front of them and build on that goodwill you have with them.

# TESTIMONIAL

*"Testimonials describe what has been, and are a promise of what is to come." Ron Kaufman*

The ultimate goal of following up after a sale, is to generate more sales, and one of the best ways is with a testimonial or case study from a satisfied customer. Customers are far more likely to purchase from someone they trust and they will also look for testimonials and research about your company's products and services. Once you've build a great relationship and sale, you should ask for referrals. Explain to your customer of any incentives your business may offer for referrals and reassure customers that everyone receives the same attention and follow-up care. We should ensure that gaining a testimonial is part of every successful sale and it's especially needed for 'game changer' sales.

*A company I worked for was criticised by our main competitor for not having a 'major London teaching hospital contract' because we couldn't 'manage' one. It was with great pleasure that I helped a major London teaching hospital write up a case study for the implementation of our product and service to their Hospital. Never again was this comment heard from our competitor and the case study was used widely as a sales tools by other salespeople.*

# AFTERWORD

My Dad, Bob, spent all his life in sales, starting off in wholesale grocery, moving to Pharmaceuticals, then medical advertising at the Lancet. As I followed in his footsteps, gaining my first Sales Representative role at 21years old, he said 'You'll never be poor in sales and will alway have an interesting life.' he was right and sales is a great job, meeting interesting people, learning about many different subjects and I've enjoyed my journey so far..... you never stop learning.

www.ingramcontent.com/pod-product-compliance
Lightning Source LLC
Chambersburg PA
CBHW070422220526
45466CB00004B/1508